Praise for *First Communion* by Mother Mary Loyola:

"This is a child's book, and a delightful one. It should have a prominent place in the spiritual library of every Catholic home, as it is written in such a fashion as to interest, instruct, and deeply move the most untutored mind and the least reverent heart. Being intended for the young, it is likewise for the old, because the charm of simplicity, and the kind intensity of a sincerely written word are qualities whose appeal is still, and ever must be, unlimited. Father and son, mother and daughter, will dwell lovingly on these innocent pages, every passage of which brims with wisdom, and love, and piety."

—The Irish Ecclesiastical Record, December 1896

"The plan is large and broad, covering all the ground with which an adult should be familiar—the needs of the soul which the Blessed Sacrament is designed to supply—the types in which God prefigured Its nature and efficacy—the Life and Death of our Lord which it summarizes and applies—the part assigned to ourselves in connection with It. On all these points ample instruction is given, sound and definite in character, yet always in such a manner as to be understanded of children, and attractive to them. At the same time there is nothing childish, and we are much mistaken if, like other well-written children's books, this do not prove even more fascinating to their elders, and if in those who use it for the instruction of others there remain not an abiding memory of what they have gained from it themselves."

—The Month, June 1896

TU ES SACERDOS IN ÆTERNUM SECUNDUM ORDINEM MELCHISEDECH. Ps. 109.

QUESTIONS

ON
FIRST COMMUNION

A GUIDE FOR CATECHISTS
BY
MOTHER MARY LOYOLA

EDITED BY
LISA BERGMAN

WITH AN INTRODUCTORY NOTE BY
HERBERT CARDINAL VAUGHAN
CARDINAL ARCHBISHOP OF WESTMINSTER

2014
ST. AUGUSTINE ACADEMY PRESS
LISLE, ILLINOIS

This book is a newly typeset edition that combines the text of the
1903 edition of *Questions on First Communion*, published by Burns & Oates,
and portions of the two-volume 1882 edition of *Catechism Made Easy*
by Rev. Henry Gibson, also published by Burns & Oates.
All editing strictly limited to the correction of errors in the original text, minor
clarifications in punctuation or phrasing, and formatting of the text for ease of use.
Any remaining oddities of spelling or phrasing are as found in the original.

No Imprimatur is found in the original text of *Questions on First Communion*.

The Imprimatur for the book *Catechism Made Easy*, from which the stories
supplied in this volume have been taken, is as follows:

Nihil Obstat
WILFRIDUS MORDAUNT,
Censor deputatus

Imprimatur
HENRICUS EDUARDUS,
Cardinalis Archiepiscopus

This book was originally published in 1903 by Burns & Oates.
This edition ©2014 by St. Augustine Academy Press.
Editing by Lisa Bergman.

ISBN: 978-1-936639-28-1
Library of Congress Control Number: 2014939436

TO THE CATECHISTS
WHO MAY USE THIS LITTLE BOOK

I HAVE ASKED Mother Mary Loyola to draw up a series of questions, so as to divide her excellent Book of Preparation for First Communion into the number of lessons that the children should receive between the beginning of Lent and Sunday within the Octave of Corpus Christi, the day for the First Communion.

This Book of Instructions, and the Questions will be of use to Priests; but I have especially in mind the Sisters, Ladies of Charity, members of the Confraternity of Christian Doctrine, and other lay persons, Masters and Mistresses, &c., who under the direction of the clergy will teach the children in small classes, as is done in Milan, Rome, and in many places in England. I have particularly before me the Cathedral of Salford, St. Patrick's, Manchester, and St. Mary's, Bayswater, where lay teachers of the Congregation have for years rendered splendid service in the Sunday schools.

I warmly commend the system of Mother Loyola's Book, *First Communion*, because it does not burden the children with a number of lessons to be learnt by heart, but really interests them, awakens their attention, and presents our Lord's Personality and Life to them in a way calculated to draw their affections to Him, and thus to prepare them in the most rational and human manner for the Sacrament they are to receive.

The Catechist, whether man or woman, must take pains to prepare beforehand, by carefully reading the lesson over at home and making himself thoroughly familiar with what he is going to teach—doing this in the spirit of an Apostle who is intent upon making our Lord's Life of love attractive to these children, whose future will depend entirely upon their having learnt to love and serve Him.

Whether the classes should be held in the Churches, which would seem to be the better plan, or in School-rooms, must depend upon circumstances, of which the Rector of the Mission is the best judge. In Rome the classes to this day are held in St. Peter's, where the Arch-confraternity of Christian Doctrine was established in 1607, nearly 300 years ago. This has the great advantage of cutting off this most religious act from what many regard as the drudgery of the school-room and of secular lessons.

Many Indulgences have been granted by the Holy See to all the faithful who act as Catechists, or teach Christian Doctrine to children, whether in Church or elsewhere.

INSTRUCTIONS FOR THE USE OF THIS BOOK

I may add just a few words of advice as to the use of the Book and of the Questions that have been drawn up, dividing it into lessons.

1. The pages that make up a lesson should be read over to the children distinctly and slowly so that they may take it all in. When the Catechist has done this and given the meaning of what has been said in his own words, and thinks the children have grasped it, he may begin to ask them the Questions here given, helping them and encouraging them to answer in their own words.

2. There being much matter to be learnt in each lesson, the Catechist, when he feels that the children cannot take it all in, should make a prudent selection of what is more important, omitting the rest. To give the mind on each occasion just as much as it can assimilate, and not more, is better than to overburden and fatigue the children by expecting too much of them.

3. The extra story should be read, or, still better, told by the Catechist in his own words, as a reward for attention and good conduct.

4. If you can get a large print, and preferably a coloured one, representing any scene in the lesson you have been giving, show it to the whole class after they have mastered the lesson, and make some of the children point out the different objects in the picture. This will serve to fix the lesson in their minds in an agreeable and easy way. It is better not to show more than one picture at each lesson.

5. Before leaving, it may be found useful to read out the subsequent lesson, that the children may know something of what they will hear again the next time they meet.

6. Every lesson ought to begin with a short prayer, and to end with singing a hymn, or with some prayer. Singing a hymn brightens up the children. If they show signs of fatigue during the lesson, the Catechist may say, "You seem tired, let us sing a few verses of a hymn."

It is a great thing to get the children to pray earnestly, and the Catechist must not hesitate through shyness to set them the example. If he can call attention to some fact of our Lord's Life in the lesson, as a motive or reason for prayer, all the better. The prayer should not be too long.

Herbert Cardinal Vaughan,
Archbishop of Westminster
Archbishop's House,
Feast of the Holy Name, 1903

FEATURES OF THIS BOOK

• Notes indicating pages covered in each lesson.

    • Page references given in the original edition of this book. These align with the page numbers of the original edition of *First Communion*.

        • Page references updated to align with the page numbers of the 2011 edition of *First Communion*.

           • Stories recommended to accompany each lesson, found in the appendix.

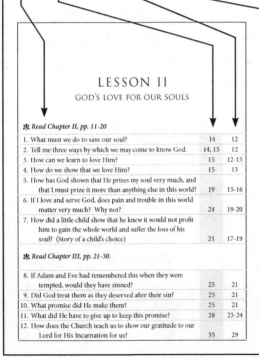

LESSON II
GOD'S LOVE FOR OUR SOULS

Read Chapter II, pp. 11-20

1. What must we do to save our soul?	14	12
2. Tell me three ways by which we may come to know God.	14, 15	12
3. How can we learn to love Him?	15	12-13
4. How do we show that we love Him?	15	13
5. How has God shown that He prizes my soul very much, and that I must prize it more than anything else in this world?	19	15-16
6. If I love and serve God, does pain and trouble in this world matter very much? Why not?	24	19-20
7. How did a little child show that he knew it would not profit him to gain the whole world and suffer the loss of his soul? (Story of a child's choice)	21	17-19

Read Chapter III, pp. 21-30.

8. If Adam and Eve had remembered this when they were tempted, would they have sinned?	25	21
9. Did God treat them as they deserved after their sin?	25	21
10. What promise did He make them?	25	21
11. What did He have to give up to keep this promise?	28	23-24
12. How does the Church teach us to show our gratitude to our Lord for His Incarnation for us?	35	29

Read Chapter IV, pp. 31-38.

13. Show how the promise to our first Parents became clearer as time went on.	37	31
14. Why were the Jews called the chosen people?	40	34
15. What were the nations called that were not God's people in this special way?	43	36
16. Were they too expecting a Redeemer? Why?	43	36

ADDITIONAL READING

St. Ignatius and St. Francis Xavier p.86
The Generous Prince p.87
Noble Answer of Sir Thomas More p.88
The Two Huntsmen p.88

EDITOR'S NOTE

This book of discussion questions was written by Mother Loyola as a guide for catechists in using her book *First Communion* in a classroom setting. It should be pointed out, however, that the lessons as she has laid them out do not always align with the chapter structure of *First Communion*; sometimes she covers two or more chapters in one lesson, and at other times she spreads one chapter over as many as five lessons. In order to make this as clear as possible for the catechist, we have added notations showing exactly which chapters and pages from the book are being discussed in each lesson.

We especially like the fact that, rather than including the answers to her questions, Mother Loyola has provided the page number on which the answer may be found. Not only does this method make it quick and easy to locate the answer, but since it therefore remains within its original context, this makes it especially conducive to a fuller discussion of the question, rather than supplying a simple one-word or one-sentence answer.

Of course, for us this meant that each answer would have to be found in our new edition and each page number painstakingly updated! And yet, we didn't want this guide to be useless to those who own an older edition of *First Communion*, so we have given two page numbers for each question: in the first shaded column are the page number references for the original edition of Mother Loyola's book. Then, to the far right, are the updated page number references as found in the 2011 edition published by St. Augustine Academy Press. (*See the diagram on the previous page.*)

Lastly, at the end of each lesson, Mother Loyola has recommended some additional stories that can be read to the children to reinforce the concepts they have learned. These stories were taken from the book *Catechism Made Easy* by Rev. Henry Gibson, a two-volume set published by Burns & Oates in 1882 and long out of print. In order to make these stories easily accessible, we have printed the recommended stories in an appendix at the end of this volume. Where no stories were recommended, we have included the sample acts of faith, hope, love, gratitude, humility, contrition and desire found on pages 407-411 of the original edition of *First Communion* (pp. 340-344 in the 2011 edition).

We devoutly hope that this volume will help teachers and parents alike to utilize Mother Mary Loyola's excellent book *First Communion* in preparing today's Catholic children for this tremendous Sacrament.

In Christ,
Lisa Bergman
St. Augustine Academy Press
April 2014

LESSON I

EARNESTNESS

🌱 *Read "To the Children," pp. xvii-xii.*

1. Who is the chief person that has to prepare us for our First Communion?	xvii	xvii
2. Why must we put our whole heart into our preparation?	xvii	xvii
3. Suppose we do not *feel* all the desire for our Lord's visit that we should like to feel, are we to be cast down or sad?	xviii	xviii
4. We can all have good will—how shall we show it?	xix	xviii-xix
5. To prepare ourselves for our Lord's coming we must ask Him to help us. Can we make up our own prayers and talk to Him in our own words?	xx	xix
6. Does He like these prayers we make up and say to Him?	xx	xix
7. Which of you can make in your own words an act of love?	xx	xix-xx
8. An act of sorrow for sin?	xx	xix-xx
9. An act of desire to receive our Lord?	xx	xix-xx

🌱 *Read Chapter I, pp. 1-10.*

10. Coifi asked: "What are we sent into this world for? Where are we going?" Which of you can answer these questions?	2	1-2
11. Why are we happier than the animals that frisk about in the sunshine?	3	2
12. Shall we get to Heaven if we take no pains to get ready?	4	3-4

ADDITIONAL READING

(These stories may be found at the back of this book.)
The Emperor's pet stag p.85
Which the greater fool? p.85

LESSON II
GOD'S LOVE FOR OUR SOULS

🌿 *Read Chapter II, pp. 11-20*

1. What must we do to save our soul?	14	12
2. Tell me three ways by which we may come to know God.	14, 15	12
3. How can we learn to love Him?	15	12-13
4. How do we show that we love Him?	15	13
5. How has God shown that He prizes my soul very much, and that I must prize it more than anything else in this world?	19	15-16
6. If I love and serve God, does pain and trouble in this world matter very much? Why not?	24	19-20
7. How did a little child show that he knew it would not profit him to gain the whole world and suffer the loss of his soul? (Story of a child's choice)	21	17-19

🌿 *Read Chapter III, pp. 21-30.*

8. If Adam and Eve had remembered this when they were tempted, would they have sinned?	25	21
9. Did God treat them as they deserved after their sin?	25	21
10. What promise did He make them?	25	21
11. What did He have to give up to keep this promise?	28	23-24
12. How does the Church teach us to show our gratitude to our Lord for His Incarnation for us?	35	29

ADDITIONAL READING

St. Ignatius and St. Francis Xavier p.86
The Generous Prince p.87
Noble Answer of Sir Thomas More p.88
The Two Huntsmen p.88

LESSON III
THE HOLY EUCHARIST AS A SACRIFICE

🌿 *Read Chapter V, pp. 39-48.*

1. What is a type?	49	40
2. Who can tell us some types of our Lord?	49	41
3. Show how each one of these was a type of Him.	49	41
4. What is sacrifice?	49	41
5. How long has sacrifice been offered to God?	49	41
6. Why is He to be worshipped by sacrifice?	50	41
7. How many kinds of sacrifice were offered in the Old Law?	53	43
8. For what ends were they offered?	53	43-44
9. How could the sacrifice of animals be pleasing to God?	53	44
10. When did these sacrifices cease to be pleasing to Him?	53	44
11. How was Melchisedech a type of our Lord?	51	42
12. Who were the Prophets?	51	42-43
13. Why was our Lord foretold by prophecy?	51	42
14. Mention some of the events of our Lord's life that were foretold hundreds of years before He came.	52	43
15. Which of the Prophets foretold the unbloody Sacrifice of the Holy Mass?	52	43-44
16. Show how the prophecy of Malachias is a prophecy of the Mass	54	44-45
17. By whom was the "clean oblation" foretold by Malachias first offered, and when?	53	44

ADDITIONAL READING

The Virtuous Page p.89
The Priest and his Altar Boys p.90
To Minister at the Altar p.92
Sir Thomas More and the Courtier p.93

LESSON IV

THE HOLY EUCHARIST AS A SACRAMENT

Read Chapter VI, pp. 49-59.

1. How was the Holy Eucharist prefigured as a Sacrament?	60	49
2. Find out eight ways in which the miraculous bread in the desert was a type of the Blessed Sacrament.	63	51
3. How were the little Hebrew children in the desert a type of First Communicants?	63	51-52
4. Why are the children expressly mentioned as having been fed by the manna?	64	53
5. How did our Lord show His love for children when He came on earth?	65	54
6. Of whom did He think when He folded the little children in His arms?	66	54
7. Why does He invite children to come to Him?	66	55
8. Who knows a second type of the Holy Eucharist as a Sacrament?	67	56-57
9. Find four ways in which the food of Elias was like the Food we receive at the altar.	69	57

Read Chapter VII, pp. 60-69.

10. Let us find out how Adam, Abel, Isaac, Joseph, Josue, Jonas, the Paschal Lamb, the Brazen serpent, were types of our Lord.	69	60

ADDITIONAL READING

The Sacrifice of Isaac p.93

LESSON V
BETHLEHEM

🌱 *Read the first half of Chapter VIII, pp. 70-76.*

1. Who can tell us about the stir there was in Bethlehem the night our Lord was born?	85	71
2. Was it because He was expected?	85	71
3. Who was looking about for a shelter that bitter night?	86	72
4. Why had our Lady and St. Joseph come to Bethlehem?	85	71
5. Where were they obliged to go?	86	72
6. What was the cave like?	86	71-72
7. Who lay there on the straw at midnight?	87	72
8. Find out some of the things that little Babe had to suffer on the first Christmas night.	87	72-73
9. Why did cold and unkindness hurt Him more than they hurt us? (Story of the little captive king)	29	24
10. Why did He suffer for us so much more than He need have suffered?	32	25
11. What were the two things our Lord came to do for us?	88	73
12. If we are poor shall we grumble when we look at the Infant Jesus in the cold crib?	90	74
13. What does the little Infant teach those who are well off?	90	75
14. Why did the rich man in the Gospel go to hell?	91	75
15. And how did poor Lazarus get to heaven?	91	75

ADDITIONAL READING

LESSON VI
EGYPT

🌿 *Read the second half of Chapter VIII, pp. 76-82.*

1. Who came into the cave to see the Holy Child?	92	76
2. What did the shepherds tell our Lady they had seen and heard?	92	76
3. Who else came to see the Infant Jesus?	92	78
4. Tell us the story of the magi.	93	78
5. What lessons can we learn from the holy magi?	94-97	78-81
6. And from cunning king Herod?	96	80-81
7. Who will best help us to get ready our Lord's resting-place in our hearts?	98	82
8. In what mystery of the Rosary can we think of the shepherds and the magi going to see the Infant Jesus?	-	-

🌿 *Read Chapter IX, pp. 83-95.*

9. Why does the Church call us all travelers "in this valley of tears"?	99	83
10. Are children travellers too, with troubles like the grown-up travellers?	99	83
11. Why did our Lord make Himself our Fellow-Traveller?	99	83
12. How do the holy magi visiting the Infant Jesus teach us to visit the Blessed Sacrament?	100	84

ADDITIONAL READING

Meekness the Proof of a Heavenly Doctrine p.97
Calumny Nobly Endured p.98

LESSON VII
NAZARETH

🌿 *Read Chapter X, pp. 96-106.*

1. Where did the Holy Family go after Herod's death?	115	97
2. Can we tell what the Holy House at Nazareth was like?	118	99-100
3. Where, probably, was St. Joseph's shop?	119	101
4. Why do we care to know all we can about those little places?	119	101
5. What was the cottage of Nazareth like inside?	120	101
6. How did our Lady spend her time?	120	101
7. And St. Joseph?	120	101
8. And the Holy Child?	121	102
9. Why is it so wonderful to think of Him doing common things like these?	121	102
10. If we had been in the Holy House at mealtimes, what should we have seen?	121	102-103
11. How do you think we should have said our grace if we had stood beside Jesus, Mary, and Joseph?	122	102
12. What was their conversation like, do you think?	122	102-103
13. Why was the little cottage of Nazareth more precious to God than all the world beside?	122	103
14. Which gave most glory to God, the adoration of the angels in heaven, or the obedience of the Child Jesus when He swept the shop, or washed the dishes, or went to His play?	122	103

ADDITIONAL READING

St. Teresa and the Divine Child p.99
St. Edmund and the Child Jesus p.100

LESSON VIII
JERUSALEM

🌿 *Read Chapter XI, pp. 107-122.*

1. Why did a Jewish boy look forward to his twelfth birthday?	128	107
2. Was the Holy Child less obedient as He grew up?	128	107
3. Where had He to go when He was twelve?	128	107
4. Who can tell us what the Temple of Jerusalem was like?	131	109-110
5. What should we have seen in the Court of the Gentiles?	132	110
6. What would a Jew have seen in the Court of the Women?	132	110-111
7. And a priest in the Court of the Priests?	133	111
8. What was there in the Holy Place?	133	111
9. And in the Holy of Holies?	133	111
10. Could we have gone into the Holy of Holies?	131	110
11. Do you know of any place holier still into which we may go as often as we like?	131	110
12. How should we behave in our churches because of their holiness?	131	110
13. Why was the Second Temple holier than the First, although it had no Ark of the Covenant?	134	112
14. Who can tell us what Jerusalem was like at the Feast of the Passover?	135, 136	113
15. What was the Passover?	233-235	198-200

ADDITIONAL READING

St. Ignatius and the Carrier   p.100

LESSON IX
HOME AND SCHOOL

🌿 *Read the first half of Chapter XII, pp. 123-128.*

1. Why did the Child Jesus let this pain come to His Blessed Mother and St. Joseph when He could easily have prevented it?	147	123-124
2. Did it pain Him to have to pain them?	146-147	123
3. How do some children treat their Parents?	148	124-126
4. What does the word "honor" mean in the Fourth Commandment?	148	1262
5. Why did our Lord show such honor to those who were infinitely beneath Him?	124	104
6. How must we *not* treat our Parents if we want to be like the Holy Child?	148	126
7. Who knows another reason why our Lord stayed in Jerusalem and sat among the children and the doctors?	149	126
8. What is the chief thing we have to learn at school?	149	126
9. Why is our Catechism lesson more important than our Arithmetic or our Geography?	149	126
10. How should we behave at Catechism?	149	126-127
11. Why is it so important that we should learn our Catechism well, and try to understand the explanation?	149	126-127

ADDITIONAL READING

LESSON X
THE HIDDEN LIFE

🌿 *Read the second half of Chapter XII, pp. 128-133.*

1. What are the two things we are told about the Childhood of our Blessed Lord?	152	128-129
2. How could the Child Jesus grow in wisdom and in grace?	152	129
3. How should *we* grow, particularly now during our preparation for First Communion?	153	129
4. Each day our Lady and St. Joseph loved their Holy Child more. Why was this?	153	129
5. How can we get them to love us more and more?	153	129
6. What kind of life did the Child Jesus lead at Nazareth?	153	130
7. Did His life become easier as He grew older?	153	130
8. Did He go on being obedient when He was grown up? Why?	154	154
9. Why is St. Joseph the Patron of a happy death?	154	130-131
10. What prayer may we say to get a happy death? (*Jesus, Mary, and Joseph, I give you*, etc.)	154	131
11. After the death of St. Joseph, what did our Lord become at Nazareth?	155	131
12. For whose sake was it that our Lord worked hard all day, and was found fault with and poorly paid?	157	132
13. If we are poor and have to work hard, what have we to comfort us?	157	132

ADDITIONAL READING

Filial Conduct of Sir Thomas More   p.103
The Undutiful Son   p.103
The Angel and the Hermit   p.104
Work and Pray, Pray and Work   p.105

LESSON XI
THE SCHOOL OF CHRIST

❧ *Read the first part of Chapter XIII, pp. 134-142.*

1. How many years did our Lord spend in the Hidden Life at Nazareth?	158	134
2. Where did He go when He left His home?	160	136
3. Which part of the Holy Land was more favoured, Judea in the south, or Galilee in the north?	162	137
4. Who were our Lord's disciples?	161	136
5. Who were the Apostles?	161	136
6. Where were most of the Apostles living when our Lord called them to follow Him?	161	136-137
7. Who can tell us what the Lake of Gennesareth was like?	162	137
8. Why is it so dear to us all?	162	137
9. What kind of men were the Twelve?	163	138
10. Who was the first called?	164	138
11. Whom did Andrew bring to our Lord?	164	140
12. What did our Lord say on seeing Simon?	165	140
13. In Hebrew, Latin, and French, what does Peter mean?	165	140
14. It is the same, then, as if our Lord had said in English—what?	165	140
15. From this time how did the other Apostles look upon Peter?	165	140
16. How do we know that they looked upon him as the first?	165, 170	140, 144

| 17. Who can say the names of the twelve Apostles? | 166-167 | 141-142 |

ADDITIONAL READING

St. Andrew the Apostle   p.105

LESSON XII
THE TWELVE

🌿 *Read the second part of Chapter XIII, pp. 142-147.*

1. Were the Twelve saints when our Lord called them?	167	142
2. What was St. Peter like then?	167	142
3. What name did our Lord give to two brothers among the Apostles, and why?	168	142
4. If any of us are "thunderers," must we say we cannot help our temper, and give up trying?	168	143
5. What does St. Ignatius say of people with hasty tempers?	168	143
6. What other fault had the Boanerges?	169	143
7. What happened one day when the Apostles were walking behind our Lord?	169	143-144
8. How did He reprove them?	169	144
9. Did they fall again into the same fault? What does this teach us?	170	144
10. Were St. Peter and St. Thomas much alike?	170	144-146
11. Our Lord prepared the Twelve Himself for their First Communion—how did He prepare them?	171	146
12. What did our Lord expect of His First Communicants when they were told of their faults?	171	146
13. What does He expect of His First Communicants now?	171	146-147
14. The Twelve had to *prepare themselves*—what does this mean?	172	147

ADDITIONAL READING

Trials of St. Perpetua p.106

LESSON XIII
JUDAS

🌿 *Read the last part of Chapter XIII, pp. 147-150.*

1. Which are the most dangerous—faults that come out, or faults that lie hidden?	172	147
2. What fault gradually got a mastery over Judas?	173	148
3. Was it a serious fault all at once?	173	148
4. How did it become serious?	173	148
5. How was Judas different from his fellow-Apostles?	173	147-148
6. Why did he not correct his faults like the rest?	173	148
7. What terrible lesson must we learn from him?	173	148
8. Why did the other Apostles love their Divine Master so dearly?	174	148-149
9. How did they repay His teaching?	174	149
10. He is our Master too—how does He teach and train us?	176	150
11. Will He forgive us again and again when we fall into faults?	176	150
12. Why may we ask St. Peter and St. John in a special way to help us to prepare our hearts for His coming?	176	150

ACTS OF FAITH

(Found on page 340 of First Communion)

J BELIEVE, my God, that You are really present in the Sacred Host I am going to receive—the same Jesus Christ, God and Man, Who was promised in Paradise—and was adored in Bethlehem by the shepherds and the Kings—Who lay in Mary's lap, and worked in Joseph's shop—Who went about doing good—and blessed the little children—Who taught from Peter's boat—and calmed the storm on the Lake—and prayed on the hill-tops for me—Who gave the Twelve their First Communion at the Last Supper—Who died upon the Cross—and rose again—and ascended into Heaven—Who will come again to judge the living and the dead—and Who has come to us meantime in the Blessed Sacrament to prepare our souls for that coming at the Last Day.

"I believe that Thou art Christ, the Son of the Living God."

"Lord, increase my faith."

LESSON XIV
OUR LORD AND MASTER

🌿 *Read Chapter XIV, pp. 151-161.*

1. How do we know that our Blessed Lord must have been very beautiful and very attractive?	177-180	151-154
2. Why did the crowds flock after Him?	181	154
3. How did He treat poor sinners?	181	154
4. And little children?	65, 181	54, 154
5. Why did the crowds cry out: "*He hath done all things well!*"?	182-183	155-156
6. What happened whenever He drew near to a town or village?	183	156
7. Who can tell us what happened one day at Naim?	184	156-157
8. What class of sick among the Jews was most to be pitied, and why?	185	157
9. Why is leprosy a figure of sin?	185	157-158
10. How did our Lord treat the poor lepers?	185	157
11. Who knows the story of Jairus and his little daughter?	186	158
12. What can we learn from this death of a child of twelve?	186	158
13. Why was the Heart of our Lord often sad as He went about doing good?	187	159
14. When He was sad and weary, where did He find rest?	188	159-160
15. What does He teach us here?	188	160
16. For whom did He pray at night on the mountain-side?	188	160

LESSON XV
INVITATION

🌿 *Look at the last pages of Chapter XIV, 160-161.*

1. Which of you would like to have knelt at His feet and held in your hands the hem of His robe?	189	160-161
2. What greater happiness than this are we to have soon?	189	160-161
3. Find out some ways in which we are better off than those who saw our Lord when He was on earth?	189	160-161
4. Those who loved Him used to invite Him to their houses—can we too invite Him?	189	160-161
(Look at the story of Zaccheus)	410	343
5. What do we call this invitation? (*A Spiritual Communion*)	-	-
6. Let us all learn the invitation: "*Jesus, Jesus, come to me!*"	-	*see over*
7. Who will remember to invite our Lord in these words every day from now to our First Communion—once in the morning and once in the afternoon? When will you say it?	-	-
8. The poor sick used to come to our Lord that He might lay His hands on their eyes, or ears, or on the dreadful sores that no one else would touch. What shall we ask Him to cure in us?	-	-

JESUS, JESUS, COME TO ME

JESUS, JESUS, come to me.
Oh! how much I long for Thee!
Come Thou, of all friends the best,
Take possession of my breast.

Chorus: Comfort my poor soul distress'd,
Take possession of my breast;
Oh! how oft I sigh for Thee—
Jesus, Jesus come to me.

Empty is all worldly joy,
Ever mixed with some alloy;
Give me, my true Sov'reign good,
Jesus, Thy own Flesh and Blood

Comfort my poor soul distress'd,
Take possession of my breast;
Oh! how oft I sigh for Thee—
Jesus, Jesus come to me.

On the Cross three hours for me
Thou didst hang in agony;
I my heart to Thee resign;
Oh! what rapture to be Thine!

Comfort my poor soul distress'd,
Take possession of my breast;
Oh! how oft I sigh for Thee—
Jesus, Jesus come to me.

LESSON XVI
THE FEEDING OF THE FIVE THOUSAND

✤ Read Chapter XV, pp. 162-171.

1. Who knows the story of the Twelve going out one day with our Lord to a desert place for a rest?	190	162
2. Did they get a rest?	190	163
3. What happened when their boat got to land?	192	163
4. How was that day spent?	193	164
5. What did our Lord teach the people?	194	165
6. When evening was come, did He send them home hungry?	195-196	166
7. The feast in the desert was the type of another Feast our Lord was going to give. Find five ways in which it was like that other Feast.	195-196	166-167
8. What did the people do when they saw what a miracle had been worked?	197	167
9. Where did the Twelve go?	197	169
10. And our Lord?	197	169
11. What happened that night on the Lake?	199-200	170
12. Why is our soul like that Lake?	200	171
13. What kind of things make a storm on our lake?	200	171
14. What are we to do when there is a storm?	200	171

ACT OF HOPE

(found on page 341 of First Communion)

WHAT can You refuse me, O my Friend and my Brother, when You give me Your very Self? You *cannot* say that anything is impossible or difficult to You. You *will* not say You have no desire to cure what is evil in my soul—and to strengthen what is good—to give me grace to keep free all my life from mortal sin—to persevere to the end—to come safely to Your Feet in Heaven. All these things, and all the blessings that You see will be good for me to have in this life—I ask You now—and believe with a firm trust that You will give me. You invite me now to come to You—You *tell* me to come to You—surely I may hope for great things from Your visit.

LESSON XVII
THE PROMISE OF THE EUCHARIST

Read the first half of Chapter XVI, pp. 172-177.

1. What lesson had the Twelve learned on that day which they thought was going to be a holiday?	201	172
2. What lesson can we learn?	201	172
3. What happened when the people found our Lord the next day?	202	173
4. How had their minds been prepared for the promise of the Eucharist?	203	173
5. Who remembers three types of the Blessed Eucharist as a Sacrament?	203	173
6. Why must we listen very attentively to the instruction our Lord gave the crowd this day?	203	174
7. Why were His listeners so eager that day to see and hear Him?	204	174
8. What did He tell them about a Bread from Heaven?	204	174
9. What was that Bread to be?	204	175
10. What words does the priest say in giving Holy Communion that remind us of the Living Bread promised that day?	204	175
11. When the people spoke of the manna in the desert, what did our Lord say?	205	175
12. Some of the Jews murmured at His words—why?	206	176

13. Do any people murmur now? Why?	206	176
14. How did our Lord threaten those who would not believe His words and receive the Divine Food He was going to give them?	206	176
15. When many of His disciples went away because of this "hard saying," as they called it, what did our Lord say?	206	176
16. Why were these Jews very foolish to murmur and leave our Lord?	206-207	176-177
17. Had He asked them to *understand* what they called a "hard saying"?	207	177
18. Can any one understand all that God does? Why not?	226	192
19. What, then, should they have done?	207	177

LESSON XVIII
"GIVE US ALWAYS THIS BREAD"

🌿 *Read the second half of Chapter XVI, pp. 177-183.*

1. Did our Lord mean to give the Jews His real true Body, the very living Body they saw before them?	208-209	177-178
2. How do we know they understood this?	208	177-178
3. If they had mistaken His meaning, what would He have done when He saw them going wrong?	210	179
4. What very solemn words did He use to show He meant exactly what His words expressed?	209	178-179
5. What did our Lord say sadly to the Twelve?	211	180
6. Why was He sad?	211	179-180
7. How did St. Peter answer our Lord's question: "Will you also go away?"	211	180
(Story of the little Protestant)	211	180
8. What heretic first denied the Real Presence of our Lord in the Blessed Sacrament? Did he dare to die denying it?	212	180
9. What did Luther say about those who denied it?	212	181
(Story of St. Jane Frances de Chantal)	213	181
10. What prayer made that day at Capharnaum may we often say now that we are preparing to receive the Divine Bread then promised? ("*Lord, give us always this Bread*")	215	182-183

ACT OF LOVE

(found on page 341 of First Communion)

I DO NOT KNOW half as much about You, dear Lord, as I shall do some day. But surely I know enough even now to love You with all my heart. I know You are infinitely beautiful and good—tender and gentle and loving—generous and forgiving—and I know that besides being so good in Yourself—You have been wonderfully good and kind to me. In return You ask only my love: "*My child, give Me thy heart.*" Take it, Lord. I give it to You—to be Yours always. Let me love You with all my heart—with all my soul—with all my mind—with all my strength. And help me to love as myself all these whom You invite to share with me this Gift of Your love.

LESSON XIX
THE REAL PRESENCE

Read the first part of Chapter XVII, pp. 184-189.

1. What does St. John tell us about the place where the promise of the Blessed Eucharist was made?	216	184
2. Is there anything remaining of the synagogue?	217	184
3. When do we all remember the good centurion?	217	185
4. What are the chief *dogmas,* or truths, respecting the Blessed Sacrament?	218	186
5. What is meant by the Real Presence?	218	186
6. Show how the Real Presence is clear from our Lord's words at Capharnaum.	205-206	175-176
7. Is it the very same Body and Blood that were in the crib at Bethlehem, that were on the Cross, that are now in Heaven?	219	186
8. Show from the words of Institution that our Lord could not have meant the consecrated Bread was a mere figure to remind us of Him.	219	186
9. Show from St. Paul's words to the Corinthians that in the Blessed Sacrament Jesus Christ is present really, truly, and substantially.	220-221	187
10. Could mere bread and wine be received unworthily?	221	188
11. What does St. Paul mean by "prove himself"?	221	188
12. "And so" let him eat?	221	188

LESSON XX
TRANSUBSTANTIATION

🌿 *Read the second part of Chapter XVII, pp. 189-192.*

1. What does the word *Transubstantiation* mean?	223	189
2. What do we mean by *substance*?	223	189190
3. Can we see or touch the substance of this book I hold in my hand?	223	190
4. What do we call those things which my senses perceive about it?	223	190
5. What do we call the thing itself?	223	190
6. Can we separate the appearances from the substance?	223	190
7. Who can separate them?	223	190
8. When does God do this?	223	190
9. What does "*trans*" mean?	223	189
10. What happens at Mass to the substance of the bread and the wine?	224	190
11. Are the Body and Blood of Christ there *together with* the bread and wine?	224	190
12. What word expresses this change of substance?	223	190
13. Our Lord once worked a miracle in which the change of substance could be perceived by the senses—when was it?	224	190
14. Why is the Transubstantiation at Mass more wonderful than its type at Cana of Galilee?	225	191

15. What reward has our Lord promised to those who believe without seeing? (Story of St. Louis)	225	191
16. Why is it very foolish to refuse to believe what we cannot understand?	226	192

CHRIST WHOLE AND ENTIRE UNDER EACH SPECIES

❧ *Read the third part of Chapter XVII, pp. 192-194.*

17. Why is the Soul of Christ with His Body and Blood?	227	192
18. Why is the Divinity there also?	227	192
19. Why is Christ present whole and entire under each species?	226-227	192
20. How does St. Paul make this clear?	227	192-193
21. Are the laity deprived of anything by receiving this Sacrament under one kind only?	227	193
22. Used they to receive under both kinds?	227	193
23. Why has the discipline of the Church changed in this respect?	227	193
24. When do priests receive under one kind only?	227	193

LESSON XXI
THE LAST SUPPER

🌿 *Read the first half of Chapter XVIII, pp. 195-203.*

1. What do we call the last week before our Lord's Passion and Death?	-	-
2. Why is the Sunday of this week called Palm Sunday?	229	195
3. What happened that day on His road to Jerusalem and in the Temple?	229	195-196
4. Where was our Lord obliged to spend the night during this week?	231	196
5. Where did He send St. Peter and St. John on the Thursday of this week?	231	196
6. What did they see on their way?	231-232	197
7. What do we call the Thursday of this week?	-	-
8. Why is that Upper Chamber to which they were sent so interesting and dear to us?	233	198
9. What should we have seen if we had been there with Peter and John?	233	198
10. What was the Feast of the Passover?	129, 138-139, 235	108, 115-116, 200
11. What was required as to the Paschal lamb?	233	198
12. Who can tell us what was done at the Paschal supper?	235	200
13. What had St. John to do as the youngest there?	236	200

LESSON XXII
INSTITUTION OF THE BLESSED SACRAMENT AND OF THE MASS

❧ *Read the second half of Chapter XVIII, pp. 203-208.*

1. How does the Beloved Disciple begin his account of the Institution of the Blessed Sacrament?	238	203
2. What did the Twelve notice about our Lord's words that night?	239	204
3. How did He prepare them for their First Communion which was now so near?	239	204
4. All First Communicants should make the acts before Communion often as the holy time draws near—Which of you can make an Act of Faith? Of Hope? Of Love? Of Contrition? Of Desire to receive our Lord?*	-	-
5. When supper was over, what did our Lord do and say as He took into His hands one of the loaves of unleavened bread?	240	204
6. And what did the Twelve do?	240	205
7. What did our Lord say over the chalice?	241	205
8. Why did our Lord give to His Apostles His precious Body and Blood for their Food?	241	205

* The sample acts from Mother Loyola's *First Communion* are found in the original edition on pages 407-411, and in the new edition on pages 340-344. They are also included in this volume: *Faith* on p.26, *Hope* on p.32, *Love* on p.36, *Contrition* on p.70, and *Desire* on p.80.

ADDITIONAL READING

To Minister at the Altar p.92

LESSON XXIII
CALVARY

🌿 *Read Chapter XIX, pp. 209-223.*

1. What did it cost our Lord to leave us this memorial of His Passion and Death—the Blessed Eucharist?	246, 262	210, 222
2. What did His Mother see when she met Him on His way to Calvary?	249	212
3. What had He suffered since He left the Supper Room?	247	210
4. Had we any share in thus disfiguring Him and spoiling all His beauty?	-	-
5. What happened along the Way of the Cross?	248-253	211-214
6. And when our Lord reached Calvary?	253	214-215
7. Why were our Lord's enemies "sore afraid" after a while?	253	215
8. For what ends did our Lord offer His bloody Sacrifice?	254	216
9. For whom was His first prayer on the Cross?	255	217
10. For whom was His Second Word?	256	217
11. And the Third Word?	256	217
12. What Word showed the anguish of His blessed Soul?	257	218
13. Why did our Lord make known to us this pain of His Soul?	258	219
14. What Word tells us of His greatest bodily torment?	259	219
15. What is the meaning of the Word: "It is finished"?	259	220
16. What does our Lord teach us by His last Word?	260	220
17. Our Lord tells us that no man can do more than to die for his friend—has He done more for us than this?	260	221

ADDITIONAL READING

LESSON XXIV
TEMPTATION

🌿 *Read Chapter XX, pp. 227-239.*

1. Our First Communion is drawing near—what has our Lord done to prepare for it?	267	227
2. What does He expect us to do by way of preparation?	267	227
3. Why does the devil hate us so much and want to hurt us?	267	227
4. How does he try to hurt us?	268	228
5. Is temptation the same as sin?	268	228
6. Why is the devil like a thief?	268	228
7. When does he knock loud?	268	228
8. And when softly?	269	228
9. Why must we never say to ourselves: "It does not matter, it is only a venial sin"?	269	229
10. Why does the devil tempt everybody to neglect prayer?	269	229
11. What is meant by the occasions of sin?	270	229
12. Which are the most common occasions of sin?	270	229
13. Why is it so dangerous to go with bad companions?	270	230
14. What is human respect?	271	230
15. How can we prevent bad example or ridicule from leading us astray?	272	230-231
(Story of the Catholic at Oxford)	280	237
16. What will keep us from giving bad example ourselves?	273	232
(Story of a young convert)	281	238

Additional Reading

Conversion of St. Ignatius Loyola p.110
St. Augustine's Experience of the Use of Good Books p.111
The Irish Servant Girl p.112

LESSON XXV

SELF-DENIAL (1)

Read Chapter XXI, pp. 240-247.

1. Does preparation for First Communion mean only listening to instructions and saying prayers? What else, then?	280	240
2. What enemy have we at home even more to be feared than the devil?	285, 286	241, 242
3. Why is our body called a servant?	286	241-242
4. Why is it a dangerous servant? (Story of the Duchess of Marlborough)	287-288	242-243
5. How must we keep it in its place?	289-290	244
6. Why have all the saints practised self-denial?	291	245
7. Which people really love their body most—those who refuse it what it should not have, or those who give it all it wants?	291-292	245-246
8. What must we do when it is hard to say "No" to ourselves?	293	247

Read the first pages of Chapter XXII, pp. 248-249.

9. When are we *bound* to deny ourselves?	294	248
10. Who can show that all our faults come from a want of self-denial?	294	248
11. Why does it please the devil to see us giving way to our bad inclinations?	295	249

ADDITIONAL READING

Daniel and his Young Companions p.113
Anecdotes of Louis XVI p.114
True Obedience p.115
The Countryman and the Vipers p.117
The Hermit and his Disciple p.117
The Hermit's answer to his Disciples p.118

LESSON XXVI
SELF-DENIAL (2)

🌿 *Read Chapter XXII, pp. 248-255.*

1. We are *bound* to deny ourselves at times—when?	294	248
2. Do we earn a reward by being patient in troubles which we cannot help?	295-296	249
3. How can we come to do this easily?	295-296	249-250
4. Besides "being crucified," St. Paul says we should "crucify ourselves." What does he mean by this?	296	249
5. Why is it very useful to deny ourselves sometimes when we are not obliged?	296	250
6. Who can tell us of some ways in which we can practice little mortifications?	296-298	250-251
7. And if we find it hard to deny ourselves, what thoughts will help us?	299-301	252-254
8. Why will the thought of the Resurrection help us?	302	254
9. If we are still afraid of self-denial, how can we gain strength against ourselves?	303-304	255

ADDITIONAL READING

Conversion of the Bulgarians   p.119
The Indian Cacique   p.120
The Bunch of Grapes   p.121

ACT OF GRATITUDE

(found on pages 341-342 of First Communion)

My God, how good You have been to me. How many things You have given me. How much more You have done for me than for millions and millions of other children who are in the world today. I have a good father and mother and a happy home. You have made me a child of Your Holy Catholic Church when I might have been one of the little Protestants I see all around me, who do not know how to get their sins forgiven, who have never heard of Your Real Presence, or of a First Communion Day. Why have You been so very good *to me?* Why have You loved me so? I cannot think why, for I am sure I have not loved You very much. What can I give You in return? David cried out in the fullness of his heart: "*What shall I render to the Lord for all He has given unto me?*" Yet David had not so much to thank You for as I have. What would David have said had he known what You are going to give *to me?* Many kings and prophets have desired to see the things I see and have not seen them, and to hear the things I hear and have not heard them. Wait till the day of my First Communion, Lord, and I will pay You all. Yes, then I will give you as much as you have ever given me—more than any favours You have ever bestowed upon me—more than the Heaven You are getting ready for me—I will give You Yourself.

LESSON XXVII
HOW TO OVERCOME TEMPTATION

Read Chapter XXIII, pp. 256-264.

1. Are we to be frightened when temptation comes? Why not?	305	256
2. But we must be prompt and courageous—what does this mean?	307	257
3. How can we get rid of a thought that teases us?	307	258
4. What should we do when the temptation has left us?	307	258
5. Why should we not hide our temptations from our confessor?	308	258
6. Why should we keep up our heart when we are tempted?	308	259
7. Why is temptation a good sign?	309	259
8. St. John saw palms in the hands of the Saints in Heaven—why?	309	259
9. Why does the devil try so hard to get us to be careless about prayer and the Sacraments?	310	260
10. Why is he glad to see us careless about little faults?	310	260
11. Why is it very foolish to be downhearted in temptation?	305-306, 311	256-257, 261
12. Who knows one reason why God allows us to be tempted?	311	261
13. If we fall in the temptation, what are we to do?	311	261
14. Are we ever to be discouraged and give up trying? Even if we fall again and again? Why not?	312	261

15. How does our Lord always treat us when we turn to Him after a fall?	312	261-262
16. How did the Saints make a good use even of their faults?	312-313	262
(A sad story)	313	262-263

📍 *Read Chapter XXIV, pp. 265-271.*

17. What do we mean by a predominant passion?	318	266
18. Why should we try to find out our predominant passion?	318, 321	266, 268
19. How do we find it out?	317-321	265-268
20. Why must we fight against our predominant passion?	323	269-270
(Story of Arabi)	322	269
21. Shall we overcome it all at once?	323	269
22. What must we do after each defeat?	323	269-270
23. Do we fight alone, or are there any watching and helping us?	323	270

ADDITIONAL READING

The Fireman's Daughter   p.121
Death rather than a Lie   p.122
The Bishop and the Soldiers   p.123

LESSON XXVIII
PREPARATION FOR CONFESSION*

Read the first part of Chapter XXV, pp. 272-279.

1. Who can tell us the parable of the Marriage feast?	326	273
2. What did our Lord mean to teach us by this parable?	327	273
3. What must we do before we come to our Lord's Table?	328	274
4. Where is the white robe to be had?	328	274
5. What kind of confession are children generally advised to make before First Communion?	332	278
6. What is a general confession?	332	278
7. When is a general confession necessary?	332	278
8. When is a confession bad?	332	278
9. What will set a bad confession right?	332	278
10. Suppose a person did not mean to make a bad confession but was afraid afterwards that it had been bad?	332	278
11. If there has not been a bad confession, is a general confession *necessary*?	333	278
12. Why may a general confession before First Communion be *useful* even when not necessary?	333	278-279
13. How may we help ourselves to remember our sins of long ago?	333	279

* This subject is more fully treated in Mother Loyola's books *First Confession* and *Forgive us our Trespasses.*

14. What must we do if we cannot remember the number of times we have fallen into a sin?	334	279

LESSON XXIX
THE FOUR THINGS (1)

1. WE MUST ASK GOD'S HELP

❧ Read the next part of Chapter XXV, pp. 275-283.

1. What are the four things we have to do to prepare for confession?	329	275
2. Why must we ask God's help?	329	275

2. WE MUST CAREFULLY EXAMINE OUR CONSCIENCE

3. Why should we follow some order in the examination of our conscience?	337-338	282
4. What order may we follow?	338	282
5. We are told to give a reasonable care to our examination of conscience—what amount of care should we think reasonable?	334	279
6. Why would it be silly to fidget over it?	334	279-280
7. What sins are we strictly bound to confess?	335	280
8. How many things must there be to make a mortal sin?	334	280
9. What does each of these three things mean?	334	280
10. Can those who are trying to serve God, and who go to confession regularly, commit a mortal sin without remembering it?	335	280

11. Suppose there were mortal sins that we had not confessed properly and which we have now forgotten?	335-336	280-281
12. Or mortal sins confessed without knowing we had not true sorrow for them?	336	281
13. Why is it well to confess in our general confession all the chief sins we can call to mind after reasonable examination?	336	281-282
14. How did our Lord show the purity of soul with which we should come to Him in Holy Communion?	336	281-282
15. What two faults have to be guarded against in the examination of conscience?	337	282

ADDITIONAL READING

The Martyr of Confession p.123

LESSON XXX
THE FOUR THINGS (2)

3. WE MUST TAKE TIME AND CARE TO MAKE A GOOD ACT OF CONTRITION

Read the next part of Chapter XXV, pp. 283-290.

1. Is examination of conscience the chief part of preparation for confession? Why not?	339	283-284
2. Why is contrition all important?	339	284
3. Suppose we had confessed without contrition every sin we had ever committed, and had had absolution?	340-341	284
4. Why is contrition like hush-money?	340	284-285
5. How are we to get contrition?	342	286
6. Is it enough to ask for it?	342	286
7. How do we do our part to secure it?	342	286
8. What do we mean by motives for contrition?	343-344	286
9. Which are the chief motives?	343	286-287
10. Why are they like a ladder?	343	287
(Story of the gentleman and the baby)	343	287
11. How will the thought of Hell or Purgatory make us sorry for our sins?	344	287
12. How will the thought of the Scourging, the Crowning with Thorns, or the Crucifixion, make us sorry?	344	287-288
13. Gratitude will lead us to contrition—how?	344	288

ADDITIONAL READING

St. Teresa's Vision of Hell p.125
The Three Stations p.127
"I weep because you do not weep" p.128

LESSON XXXI
THE FOUR THINGS (3)

4. WE MUST RESOLVE TO RENOUNCE OUR SINS AND TO BEGIN A NEW LIFE FOR THE FUTURE

❦ *Read the next part of Chapter XXV, pp. 290-291.*

1. What is the purpose of amendment we are bound to have?	348	290
2. What is a good resolution to make in each confession?	348	291
3. How can we tell what fault to pick out for our purpose of amendment?	348	290-291
4. There are three things we should resolve to do with each confession—what are they?	348	291
5. Sometimes there is a duty to make satisfaction to our neighbour—when?	348	291
6. Does it always show we have not had a firm purpose of amendment, if we fall into the same faults again and again? Why not?	348	291
7. What must we try to do with regard to these faults?	348	291
8. What two things make preparation for confession very simple and easy?	338	283
9. As soon as we get into church, what should we do?	338	283
(Story of the boys preparing for confession)	338	283

🪷 *Read Chapter XXVI, pp. 298-302.*		
10. Who can tell us the parable of the lost sheep?	357	298
11. Why was the sheep so silly as to leave the fold?	357	298
12. When are we silly like that sheep?	-	-
13. Is it ever nice to have our own way like the sheep?	-	-
14. For how long is it nice? And then?	-	-
15. The sheep got into a thicket and struggled hard to get out. Are we ever like it?	358	299
16. What did the poor sheep do when it heard the wolf coming?	359	299-300
17. What must we do when we have wandered from the Good Shepherd?	359	300
18. Why does our Lord call Himself the Good Shepherd?	359	300
19. How does the Good Shepherd seek us His sheep?	359	300
20. What has it cost Him to save us?	360-361	300-301
21. What lessons do we learn from this parable?	361-362	301-302

ADDITIONAL READING

There is Mercy for Every Sin   p.129
The Prodigal Son   p.130
Naaman Cured of his Leprosy   p.131

LESSON XXXII
CONFESSION

🌿 *Read the last part of Chapter XXV, pp. 291-297.*

1. Suppose we have any difficulty in telling a sin, what should we do?	349	291
2. Should we ever hide anything that troubles our conscience?	349	291
3. Or leave it to be said at some future time?	349	291
4. What will help us to make a brave effort?	349	291
5. And what will our Lord give us in return?	349	291-292
6. When we have confessed our sins, what must we do?	349	292

AFTER CONFESSION

7. Returning to our place, what should we do?	349-350	292
(Story of the African slave)	351	293
8. When did our Lord institute the Sacrament of Penance?	354	295
9. What should this teach us?	354	295-296
10. Why is this Sacrament called the Sacrament of Mercy, and a second plank after shipwreck?	354	295-296
11. Which are the two feet by which the children of the Church march along on the road to Heaven?	355	296
12. Why do some get on so much faster than others?	355	296

ADDITIONAL READING

False Humility p.133

LESSON XXXIII
WHO COMES?

❧ *Read Chapter XXVII, pp. 304-313.*

1. What is wanted to make us grateful to our Lord who comes so far to visit us?	366-367	306-307
(Story of the boy going home for the holidays)	363	304-305
2. How do we increase our faith?	367-368	307-308
3. The shortest way to get all the dispositions we want is to increase our faith—Why?	368-371	308-310
4. What book will help us to increase our faith, and help us all our life in God's service if we get to know and love it?	373	311
5. Is it sometimes our own fault that we have no feelings of devotion? When?	371	310
6. Suppose we have been somewhat careless during our preparation for First Communion and now are cold and dry—what must we do?	372	311
7. Which of you can make in your own words an Act of Hope or Love?	-	-
(Urban's Act of Hope)	373	312
8. Now that the time of our First Communion is so near, what should we do to make our hearts pleasing to our Lord?	374	312-313
9. Why is it well to have a method in our preparation for Holy Communion?	374	313

ADDITIONAL READING

The Power of Prayer   p.133
The Thundering Legion   p.135

LESSON XXXIV
TO WHOM DOES HE COME?

Read Chapter XXVIII, pp. 314-321.

1. We expect people to keep their place—What will help us to keep our right place before God?	377	315
2. Have we any reason to be proud even of our good works? Why not?	377-379	315-316
(Story of the baby-boatman)	378	316
3. Why does God hate pride so much?	379, 383	316, 319
4. How is it the Saints could be so humble?	380-381	317-318
5. What have we more than our nothingness to make us ashamed?	381	318
6. Who knows a good way of getting rid of proud thoughts?	382	318
7. Should the thought of our sins and weakness make us discouraged or unhappy? Why not?	382	319
8. Humility we must all have if we are to get to Heaven—how are we to learn it?	383-384	320
9. How will our Lord's example help us to be like Him, meek and humble of heart?	384	320

ADDITIONAL READING

Conversion of St. John Gualbert p.136

ACT OF HUMILITY

(found on page 342 of First Communion)

I THINK it ought to be very easy for me to be humble—for, first, I have nothing to be proud of—and next, I have plenty to be ashamed of. My God, all that I have of good You have given me. I have nothing of my own, but my sins. And how many sins there have been. I have been so naughty, so careless, so ungrateful. St. Elizabeth was surprised that our Lady should come to see her. St. Peter cried out: "Depart from me, for I am a sinful man, O Lord." The pagan centurion said, "Lord, I am not worthy." And I too wonder that the God of Heaven and earth should come to me. I will not say, "Depart from me," but I do say with all my heart: "Lord, I am not worthy that Thou shouldst come under my roof."

"O God, be merciful to me, a sinner."

LESSON XXXV
WHY DOES HE COME?

Read Chapter XXIX, pp. 322-337.

1. Our Lord is coming and longing to come. Those who love us in Heaven long to see Him with us—Why?	386-387	322-323
2. Why is it very dangerous to let little faults go unchecked?	387	323
3. Why is the devil afraid of those words: "Behold, I come"?	387	323
4. How does the Holy Eucharist cure what is evil in us?	389	324
(Story—Going to the doctor)	389	324-325
5. Why ought we to be glad to have our Lord for our Physician?	390	325
6. What can we tell Him about our sick souls?	391	326
7. Besides healing our souls, the Holy Eucharist nourishes them—How does It do this?	394-397	329-332
(Story of Peggy)	395	330-331
(Story of the young soldier)	398	332-333
(Story of the Indian boy)	400	334-336
8. Who will remember and say sometimes the Spiritual Communion of the Indian boy?	403	336-337

Additional Reading

St. Monica and the Servant Maid p.137

An Indian Chief on Drunkenness p.138

ACT OF CONTRITION

(found on pages 342-343 of First Communion)

*M*Y sins have made me most unworthy. But I am sorry for them—very sorry for them. I am sorry, because of all the harm they have done to my soul—more still because they have cost You so much, dear Lord—because they hurt You so much in Your Passion—they tortured Your Heart in the Garden of Olives—they stung You in the scourges—they pricked You in the thorns—they drove the nails into Your Hands and Feet. I am sorry for my sins, because they crucified You, my Saviour. And most of all I am sorry, because they have offended You, Who are so good in Yourself, so infinitely good. My God, I think perhaps You might be good to others without being infinitely good, but You must be infinitely good to be good *to me*. And so I am sorry with all my heart for having displeased You.

LESSON XXXVI
"COME, LORD JESUS!"

🌿 *Read Chapter XXX, pp. 338-354.*

1. How did the maidens prepare themselves to appear before King Assuerus?	404	338
2. The King of kings expects us to prepare our souls for Him—what is meant by sufficient preparation, or dispositions?	405	339
3. Suppose any one after going to confession were to fall into mortal sin, would it be enough to make an Act of perfect contrition, and so go to Holy Communion?	405-406	339
4. What dispositions are very good?	406	339-340
5. And what are perfect?	406-407	340
6. What are the chief Acts we should make before Communion?	407-410	340-343
7. How did our Blessed Lord show when He was on earth that He loves to be desired?	410	343
8. What are the dispositions of the body?	412, 417	345, 348
9. What is the law of the Church as to fasting before Communion?*	413	345
10. What kinds of things would not break the fast?	413	345

---

* At the time the book *First Communion* was written, the Eucharistic fast began at midnight. This requirement has since been changed (in most places) to one hour before receiving.

ADDITIONAL READING

First Communion of the Blessed Imelda p.138
Viaticum of St. Juliana p.140

LESSON XXXVII
OUR FIRST COMMUNION

❧ *Read Chapter XXXI, pp. 355-365.*

1. When we wake in the morning, what shall we do?	425	355
2. What shall we think about whilst dressing?	425	355
3. How soon should we be in church?	426	355-356
4. What is the best immediate preparation we can make?	426	356
5. What prayers are we going to say?	426	356
(Story of Winnie)	426	356
6. After Holy Communion what Acts should we make?	427	357
7. Let us see if we can make these Acts of Adoration, Thanksgiving, Love, Contrition, and Petition, now, that we may be able to make them then before we take up our book.	-	-
8. Who can make an Act of *Adoration*?	428	357
9. Whom shall we ask to help us in our Adoration?	428	357
10. Now who can make an Act of *Thanksgiving*?	429	358
11. On whom shall we call again to help us to thank our Lord?	430	360
12. What is the grandest thanksgiving we can offer?	431	360-361
13. Our chief Act must be *Love*. What can we say as we hold fast Him whom we love?	431	361
14. Why will it be easy to love Him then?	432	361

ADDITIONAL READING

LESSON XXXVIII
"STAY WITH US"

🌿 *Read the first part of Chapter XXXII, pp. 366-375.*

1. Who can tell us the story of the sad disciples on the way to Emmaus?	438-441	366-368
2. Why did their Fellow-Traveller call them foolish and slow of heart?	441	368
3. Does He ever reprove us when He comes to visit us?	441	369
4. When did He once rebuke St. Peter severely?	442	369
5. Is reproof, then, a sign of unkindness, or of confidence and love?	443	370
6. Why is it so necessary that we should come to know our faults?	443	370
(Story of the class of babies)	443	370
7. Should we be cross, then, with those who help us to know them?	444	370-371
8. How does our Lord reprove us?	444	371
9. Why must we always listen to His voice speaking to us in our conscience?	445	371
10. Does He speak to us in other ways?	445	371-372
11. Why is it wrong to give way to discouragement?	446	372
12. What did our Lord teach the two disciples about suffering?	447	373

13. What happened at the door of the inn and when they were at table?	447	373

ADDITIONAL READING

St. Francis of Sales and the Old Man   p.142
The "Enchanted Bread" of the Christians   p.143

LESSON XXXIX
"GIVE US ALWAYS THIS BREAD"

❧ *Read the last pages of Chapter XXXII, pp. 375-378.*

1. Our Communions ought to be frequent and fervent— why frequent?	450-451	375-376
2. What did the Communions of the Saints do for them?	451	376
3. What will our Communions do for us?	451	376-377
4. How can we prevent our hearts from growing cold after our First Communion?	452-453	377-378
5. What is the best thanksgiving for our First Communion?	454	378

❧ *Read the first half of Chapter XXXIII, pp. 379-386.*

6. What do we mean by perseverance?	455	379
7. What promise does our Lord make to those who persevere to the end?	455	379
8. Why was He so sad the day the little Jewish children sang "Hosanna" to Him?	456	379
9. Our Lord knows how we shall welcome Him when He comes again. Is our next welcome and our next going to be something for Him to look forward to?	456-457	380
10. How shall we obtain the grace of final perseverance?	457	382
(Story of Effie)	458	382-385

11. How shall we get the grace to keep the promises we have made to our Lord?	461	385
12. Why is holy fear a great means of perseverance?	462	385-386

ADDITIONAL READING

The First Communion Veil p.143
The Devout Communicant p.145

LESSON XL
THE FOUR LAST THINGS

🌿 *Read the second half of Chapter XXXIII, pp. 386-395.*

1. The remembrance of the Four Last Things will help us to persevere. Which do you think will help us most in time of temptation?	463	386
2. When we come to die, how shall we wish to have lived?	466	388
3. How must I go to the Sacraments all my life through, if I want them to keep me safe to the end?	467	389
4. Why shall I be glad at death if I have often thought of death during life?	467	390
5. What must I be careful about in all my confessions if I want to have nothing to trouble my conscience when I come to die?	468	390
6. Who remembers about the lamps?	467-468	389-390
7. Four things will help me to a happy death—what are they?	469	391
8. Does the thought of death make us sad or gloomy?	470	391
(Stories of St. Philip Neri)	470	391-394
9. St. Philip's asking *"And then?"* helped Francesco—how may it help us?	473	394

ADDITIONAL READING

Death makes No Distinction p.145
Story of Josaphat p.146

ACT OF DESIRE

(found on page 344 of First Communion)

J AM POOR and weak and unworthy to come to You, dear Lord—and yet I do so want to come. Do not think the desire is all on Your side— for I do indeed love and long for You. You know all things. You know, Lord, that I love You. David said: "*As the hart panteth after the water-brooks, so panteth my soul after Thee, O God.*" I wish I could long for You like that. Your loving words and ways make me desire You. And You like to come to those who desire You. Because Zacheus wanted so much to see You, You gave him more than He hoped for—not only one glance at Your beautiful Face as You passed him under the sycamore-tree, but the sound of Your voice, and Your Blessed Presence in his house, with all the change in him that Presence wrought.

And how You liked to go to Bethany, to the two sisters there, who were always looking forward to Your coming. I wish I could receive You and make You welcome as they did. Martha spared no trouble in getting ready for You. She made the house clean and tidy, and bright with flowers, and prepared all she could think of to show You honour. Help me to be like her—not cold now, nor careless—but loving and diligent. And Mary sat at Your Feet and heard Your words. So let me listen to You when You come to me in all the Communions of my life. You will speak to my heart, if only I will listen: "*Speak, Lord, for Thy servant heareth.*"

LESSON XLI
"HE THAT EATETH THIS BREAD SHALL LIVE FOREVER"

❦ *Read Chapter XXXIV, pp. 396-411.*

1. What does the Beloved Disciple tell us he saw in Heaven?	476	396-397
2. What is waiting for us there?	477	397-398
3. In Holy Communion we receive a pledge of that glory and of that joy—what does this mean?	478	398
4. What do our Lord's words *"Hold fast"* mean?	479	399
5. Why do all the Blessed carry palms?	479	399
6. How are we to get our palms?	479	399-400
(Story of Tommy)	480	400-402
7. Why is it unsafe to do as little as ever we can to get to Heaven?	483	402
8. How can we get a high place there?	485	403-404
9. What must we do now to make our Lord say to us *"Come"* when we meet Him at Judgment?	488	406
10. What can we do *now* to shorten the weary waiting of Purgatory?	489-490	406-408
11. Purgatory over at last—where shall we be taken; whom shall we see?	491-493	408-409

ADDITIONAL READING

The Martyrs of Japan p.147

St. Felicitas and her Seven Sons p.148

ADDITIONAL READING (CONT'D)

STORIES

FOR

ADDITIONAL READING

THE EMPEROR'S PET STAG

A certain Roman emperor had a favourite stag which he had succeeded in taming, and which had become much attached to its imperial master. During the day it roamed at large in the neighbouring forests, but returned at certain times to the palace to receive its food. Fearful that it might go astray, and that he might lose an animal which he prized so much, the emperor placed round its neck a golden collar bearing the inscription, "Touch me not; I belong to Caesar." No one, he thought, would dare to steal or injure it when they perceived that he had marked it for his own.

Now, Almighty God has acted to us in the same way as the Roman emperor to his pet stag. He has stamped his Divine image on our souls; our will, our memory, our understanding, our whole soul, all bear the mark that we come from God and belong to God. When, therefore, the devil presumes to attack us, let us bid him begone, saying, "Touch me not; I belong to God."

WHICH THE GREATER FOOL?

Many years ago there was a certain lord who kept a fool in his house, as many great men did in those days for their amusement. Now this lord had given the fool a staff, and charged him to keep it, till he met with one that was a greater fool than himself, bidding him, if he met with such a one, to deliver the staff to him. Not many years after, the lord fell sick, and, indeed, was sick unto death. His fool came to see him, and the sick lord told him that he must shortly leave him. "And where art thou going?" said the fool. "Into another world," said the lord. "And when wilt thou return; in a month?" "No," said the lord. " In a year?" "No." "When, then?" "Never, never!" "And what provision hast thou made," said the fool, "for thy entertainment in the place where thou art going?" "Alas! none at all." "What!" said the fool, "none at all? Here, take my staff. Art thou going to dwell there for ever, and hast made no orders for thy entertainment in a place from which thou wilt never return? Take my staff, for I am not guilty of any such folly as this."

ST. IGNATIUS AND ST. FRANCIS XAVIER

At the time when St. Ignatius was pursuing his studies at Paris, he became acquainted with Francis Xavier, a gay young nobleman who happened to be studying at the same college. Ignatius, perceiving the noble qualities of mind and heart which his young friend possessed, was bent upon gaining him to God; but as Xavier was at that time occupied only with thoughts of ambition and a desire of distinguishing himself in the world, Ignatius found that all his good advice was unavailing. He therefore contented himself with repeating to Xavier, from time to time, the words of our Lord, "What will it profit a man if he gain the whole world and suffer the loss of his own soul?" Francis, who had at first treated the advice of Ignatius with contempt, and rallied him on his devout and mortified life, began at length seriously to reflect on the words which his friend so often repeated. Applying them to his own case, he began to ask himself what indeed it would profit him to obtain all his ambitious desires, if in the end he lost his soul amid the dangers of the world. This consideration made so deep an impression on his mind that, following the impulse of grace, he put himself under the direction of St. Ignatius, entered the Society of Jesus, and became an illustrious saint and the apostle of the Indies.

THE GENEROUS PRINCE

A certain great monarch had a favourite nobleman, whom he had raised from an obscure condition, loaded with riches and honours, and placed in one of the highest offices of his kingdom. Unfortunately this favourite allowed the poison of pride to enter his heart. Puffed up with his good fortune, and not content to be second in the kingdom, he wished to be first. He accordingly planned a vast conspiracy, by which he might be able to put aside the king and take possession of the throne. Fortunately, the plot was discovered at the moment fixed for its execution. The ungrateful nobleman was stripped of his riches and dignities, and banished with all his family to a remote province, where he was reduced to the same low and destitute state from which the king had first raised him.

Now it happened that the king had a son, a noble youth, full of tender compassion and generosity. Hearing of the disgrace of the former favourite, he hastened to his father, threw himself at his feet, and with many tears implored him to pardon the exile and his family. The king graciously consented, and immediately the young prince, disguising himself, set off, alone and on foot, to bear to the wretched family the happy and unexpected tidings. After enduring the severest hardships and sufferings on the journey, the prince at length arrived at the distant province to which they had been banished. He found the exile and his family plunged in the deepest misery, and suffering the extremity of want. The generous prince hastened to console them. "Rejoice," said he; "your sufferings are now at an end. I am the son of the king who sent you into banishment, and I have implored and obtained your pardon from my father. Henceforward consider me as your friend, your brother. You shall return to court, you shall dwell in my palace, you shall sit at my own table; my riches, my honours, the kingdom which is my inheritance, all shall be yours."

At these words the unhappy exile and his family appeared in a moment restored to a new life. They raised their eyes to heaven, and blessed God for his wonderful goodness. Then, with bursting hearts and tears of gratitude, they cast themselves at the prince's feet, and strove to thank him for a generosity and self-devotion which the world had never yet beheld. But all they could utter were these simple words:—"Prince, what are we, and what art thou!"

NOBLE ANSWER OF SIR THOMAS MORE

When Sir Thomas More, the learned and pious chancellor of England, had been condemned to death by King Henry VIII for refusing to acknowledge the King's supremacy, he was visited before his execution by his wife Louisa, who, with prayers and tears, besought him to yield, assuring him that the King would, in that case, consent to spare his life. "Tell me, Louisa," said the noble confessor of the faith, "how many years could I, who am an old man, expect to live?" "You might live," she answered, "for as many as twenty years." "Oh, foolish woman," replied her husband; "and do you want me for twenty years of this miserable life on earth to forfeit an eternity of happiness, and condemn myself to an eternity of torments?"

THE TWO HUNTSMEN

Two young men had agreed to go out hunting together upon a certain Holyday of obligation, but only one of them took care to hear Mass before starting upon the expedition. They had scarcely been out an hour, when suddenly the sky grew dark, and a fearful storm came on, accompanied by such terrible peals of thunder and such vivid flashes of lightning, that it appeared as if the end of the world was approaching. But what alarmed them most was that, in the midst of the tumult of the elements, they heard from time to time a voice of thunder saying, "Strike, strike." At length the storm began to clear off, and they resumed their way, when suddenly the thunder pealed forth afresh with great fury, and the huntsman who had failed to hear Mass that morning, was struck dead on the spot by a flash of lightning. His companion, beside himself with terror, knew not which way to turn, and his terror was increased when he heard the same voice repeating, "Strike! strike the other also." At these words he was ready to sink upon the ground in mortal anguish, but his courage returned when he heard another voice reply, "I cannot strike him, for he has heard this morning the '*Verbum caro factum est*—The Word was made flesh.'" These words, my dear children, are, as you know, the concluding words of the last Gospel, at which all the congregation bend their knee in honour of our Lord's Incarnation.

THE VIRTUOUS PAGE

St. Elizabeth, Queen of Portugal, had in her service as page, a pious and faithful youth, whom she was accustomed to employ in the distribution of her alms. One of his fellow pages, filled with envy at the confidence reposed in him, determined to effect his ruin, and accordingly suggested to the king that he was regarded with too much favour by the saintly queen. The slander was believed and the king, stung with jealousy, resolved to take away the life of the page. For this purpose he gave orders to the master of a limekiln, that if on a certain day he should send to him a page to inquire whether he had executed the king's commands, he should at once seize him and cast him into the furnace, for that he had been guilty of a grievous crime, and deserved death. On the day appointed he called for the youth, and having given the message that had been agreed upon, he sent him to deliver it.

Now it happened that the page, on his way to the kiln, passed by a church at the very moment when the bell was ringing for the Elevation. As it had always been his pious custom in such a case not to pass on until the Holy Sacrifice was ended, he entered the church, and knelt down to hear the remainder of the Mass. When it was concluded, reflecting that he had not heard an entire Mass that day according to his usual practice, he remained in the church and heard two other Masses in succession.

Meanwhile the king became impatient to know whether his designs had succeeded, and by a wonderful Providence of God, despatched the accuser himself to inquire whether his orders had been executed. This being the very message agreed upon with the master of the kiln, the unhappy youth was immediately seized and, in spite of all his remonstrances, cast amid the burning lime where he was quickly consumed.

As soon as the Masses were concluded, the page who had been first despatched, hastened on to deliver his message. Upon inquiring whether the king's orders had been executed, he was told that they had, and he returned with this message to the king. The latter, seeing him return, was struck with fear and amazement, and upon hearing the circumstances, perceived at once the innocence of the page, and admired the Justice and Providence of God, who, while he protected and preserved the virtuous page, allowed the very punishment designed for him to fall on the head of his wicked calumniator.

THE PRIEST AND HIS ALTAR BOYS

There lived in the thirteenth century in the Convent of Santarem, in Portugal, a holy priest named Bernard, who was a member of the Order of St. Dominic. Being placed in care of the sacristy, he had under his charge two boys of tender age and extraordinary innocence, whom he taught to serve at Mass, and also instructed in their catechism and the rudiments of grammar. Their docility and good conduct made them very dear to him, and he did all in his power to bring them up in piety, and in tender love for the

Blessed Sacrament and the Holy Mother of God. Each morning when the boys came from their homes, they brought with them a piece of bread and a little fruit, to eat when the services were ended, and they were accustomed to take it at the foot of an image of the Blessed Virgin with the Divine Infant in her arms. The children never failed to salute respectfully the Infant Jesus, and He, to reward their innocence and piety, on one occasion descended from his mother's arms, and begged them to give him a portion of their food. Transported with joy, they gave him what he asked, and from that time they always invited the Divine Infant to partake of their frugal meal. At length they determined to acquaint Father Bernard with what had happened. "Father," said they, "the Child who rests in the arms of the Mother of God, eats daily with us, but he never brings food himself to share with us; what ought we to do?" Bernard heard with holy awe the children's story, and thus replied to them, "My dear boys, when the child comes and speaks to you to-morrow, say without fear, "Lord, Thou deignest every morning to partake of our meal, but we receive no morsel from Thy hand. We pray Thee invite us and our Father Bernard to dine with Thee in Thy Father's house.'"

The children did not fail to do as their teacher had instructed them. On the following day again the Divine Infant sat down between them to share their meal. They then made known their petition to him, begging him to invite them and their teacher to a Feast in his Father's house. The Holy Child accepted their petition with joy, and said, "You could not give me a greater pleasure than by asking this. Yes, I invite you as you desire. Tell your master that he may prepare himself by the Feast of the Ascension. On that day I will entertain you all three." In great delight the children hurried away to inform Father Bernard of the invitation they had received. That holy man, convinced of the truth of the revelation, left nothing undone to prepare himself with the greatest piety to partake of the Divine Feast.

At length the Ascension arrived, and Father Bernard, having prepared himself for the Holy Sacrifice with unusual fervour, proceeded to the altar to say Mass, attended by his two servers. To the spectators his face appeared to shine like that of an Angel, so great was the fire of Divine Love and holy desire which burnt within him. When Mass was concluded, he prostrated himself upon the altar steps, and signed to the two boys to do the same. While they thus poured forth their souls in prayer, a sweet sleep overcame them, and so they went to the Heavenly Feast of eternal life.

When the brethren of the Convent, as was their wont, went to the church to pray after their midday meal, they perceived the three bodies prostrate at the foot of the altar.

The priest was still clad in his vestments, the boys in their white surplices, and the faces of all three shone with heavenly beauty. At first it was believed that they slept, but it was soon discovered that they were dead. Whereupon the confessor of Father Bernard, to whom the latter had made known the heavenly invitation, related in presence of the whole community what had happened to the children, and what the Divine Infant had promised them. Their funeral rites were celebrated with joy and thanksgiving, and the events connected with their death were inscribed upon the stone which was erected over their common grave.

TO MINISTER AT THE ALTAR
THE GREATEST OF HONOURS

St. Wenceslaus, king of Bohemia, was celebrated for his extraordinary devotion to the Blessed Sacrament. Not content with assisting daily at several Masses, kneeling with reverence on the bare pavement, he esteemed it an exceeding honour to serve Mass in person, and to be employed in any way in the service of the altar. Thus for example, he tilled with his own hands the ground, in which he afterwards sowed the wheat that was destined to be employed in making the altar breads for the Holy Sacrifice. When the grain was ripe, he reaped and ground it, and made the breads which were afterwards to be consecrated. In like manner he gathered the grapes and made the wine which was used at Mass. Not content with spending during the day hours in prayer before the Blessed Sacrament, he often rose at night, and drawn by the sweet power of Divine love, hastened to the church to visit his hidden God. No wonder that his countenance on such occasions appeared all on fire, and the flames of love, which consumed his soul, so communicated themselves to his body, that the page who accompanied him, by treading in his footsteps, no longer experienced cold, though the ground was thick with snow.

SIR THOMAS MORE AND THE COURTIER

Sir Thomas More, the celebrated Lord Chancellor of England, took great delight in serving at Holy Mass, and though his time was much taken up with affairs of state, he frequently served several in succession. Upon one occasion a certain courtier, sadly deficient in lively faith, represented to him that King Henry would be displeased at his lowering himself to fulfill the office of a mere acolyte. "Surely," replied the Chancellor, "the king cannot be displeased at the homage which I offer to his King."

SACRIFICE OF ISAAC

"After these things God tempted Abraham, and said to him, *Abraham, Abraham,* And he answered, *Here I am.* He said to him, *Take thy only-begotten son Isaac, whom thou lovest, and go into the land of Vision, and there thou shalt offer him for a holocaust upon one of the mountains which I will show thee.*

"So Abraham rising up in the night, saddled his ass, and took with him two young men and Isaac his son; and when he had cut wood for the holocaust, he went his way to the place which God had commanded him.

"And on the third day, lifting up his eyes, he saw the place afar off. And he said to the young men, *Stay you here with the ass; I and the boy will go with speed as far as yonder, and after we have worshipped, will return to you.*

"And he took the wood for the holocaust, and laid it upon Isaac his son, and he himself carried in his hands fire and a sword. And as the two went on together, Isaac said to his father, *My father,* and he answered, *What wilt thou, son? Behold,* saith he, *fire and wood; where is the victim for the holocaust?* And Abraham said, *God will provide himself a victim for an holocaust, my son.* So they went on together.

"And they came to the place which God had shown him, where he built an altar, and laid the wood in order upon it; and when he had bound Isaac his son, he laid him on the altar upon the pile of wood. And he put forth his hand and took the sword to sacrifice his son.

"And behold an angel of the Lord from heaven called to him, saying, *Abraham, Abraham.* And he answered, *Here I am.* And he said to him, *Lay not thy hand upon the boy, neither do thou anything to him; now I know thou fearest God, and hast not spared thy only-begotten son for my sake.* Abraham lifted up his eyes, and saw behind his back a ram amongst the briers, sticking fast by the horns, which he took and offered for a holocaust instead of his son."

ST. ELIZABETH AND THE LEPER

We read in the life of St. Elizabeth, the pious duchess of Thuringia, that it was her greatest delight to minister to the wants of the sick, whom she visited and waited on in person, relieving them and dressing their loathsome sores with her own hands. Those who were the most afflicted and abandoned, were often received by her into the castle of Wartbourg, where she dwelt with her husband Louis, so that their palace usually resembled a hospital on account of the number of sick whom it contained. The good duke was not, however, displeased at her charity, for he loved her dearly, and was gentle and compassionate like herself.

Now it happened one day, when Louis was absent from home on a journey to some other part of his dominions, that there came to the castle gate a poor leper named Elias, who was covered from head to foot with putrid sores. St. Elizabeth, seeing his sad condition, received him with the tenderest charity, washed his sores with her own hands, and anointed them with a healing balm; she then sought for some vacant room in which she might place him. Finding, however, that every spare chamber was already occupied with her patients, she conducted him to her own apartment, and placed him in the very bed in which she and her husband slept.

Meanwhile the duke unexpectedly returned, and was met at the castle gate by his mother, the duchess Sophia, who loudly complained to him of the folly of his saintly wife, who, she said, had placed a dirty filthy leper in his own bed. On hearing this, Louis could not help feeling for the moment some annoyance, and he followed his mother in silence to the chamber where the leper lay. Upon approaching the bed, and drawing aside the curtains, Almighty God opened, as the historian tells us, the eyes of his soul, and he saw before him, no longer the person of the leper Elias, but the figure of Jesus crucified. Overcome with awe, he threw himself on his knees, and tears of devotion flowed from his eyes, as he gazed upon the deathlike form, the crowned head, and the bleeding wounds of his crucified Lord. Then turning to Elizabeth he said, "I pray thee, my dear sister, give often my bed to such guests as these, and be not hindered in the exercise of thy charity." Then he added, "Lord have mercy on me, a poor sinner, and make me a man according to thy own heart."

Thus did our Lord show the saintly Elizabeth and her pious husband how those who tend upon and relieve his sick, in very truth minister to his own person.

ST. MARTIN AND THE BEGGAR

St. Martin of Tours, in the early part of his life, followed the military profession, and served in the army of the Roman Emperor. His parents were idolaters, but Martin, though not yet baptised, had placed himself under instruction, and cherished in his heart an ardent desire of embracing the Christian religion.

One day in the midst of a very hard winter, as he was marching with other officers and soldiers, he met at the gates of Amiens a poor man almost naked and trembling with cold, who was begging alms of the passers by. Martin, seeing that those who went before him took no notice of this miserable object, looked upon him as reserved for himself. His numerous charities had, however, exhausted all his means, and he had nothing left but his arms and the clothes on his back. Whereupon he drew his sword, cut his cloak in two pieces, and gave one to the beggar, reserving the other for himself. Some of the bystanders laughed at the figure he made, while others were ashamed of not having relieved the poor man. The following night Martin saw in his sleep Jesus Christ, dressed in the half garment which he had given in charity, and was told by our Lord to look well at it, and see whether he knew it. He then heard Jesus say to a troop of Angels that surrounded him, "Martin, yet a catechumen, hath clothed me with this garment." This vision inspired him with fresh ardour, and determined him speedily to receive Baptism.

THERE IS NO NEED TO COUNT OUR ALMS

A noble Roman lady, named Melania, coming to visit the Abbot St. Pambo in his monastery in Egypt, brought with her three hundred pounds weight of silver which she presented to him, begging him to accept a portion of the wealth with which God had blessed her. The holy man was sitting at his work, making mats, when she arrived, and without interrupting his labour, or looking at her or her offering, contented himself with saying that God would reward her charity. Then turning to his disciple he said, "Take and distribute it among the poorest monasteries." The lady stood still, expecting that he would take some further notice of so considerable a present, but as he still went on with his work without ever glancing at the chest of money, she at length said, "Father, I do not know whether you are aware that there are three hundred pounds weight of silver in that chest." "Daughter," replied the Saint, without taking his eyes off his work, "He to whom you have made the offering, knows very well how much it weighs without your telling him. If, indeed, you had given it to me, there might be some reason to inform me of the weight; but if you really intended it as a present to God, who did not disdain the poor widow's mite, do not say any more about it." So saying, he dismissed her, much edified with the lesson she had received.

MEEKNESS THE PROOF OF A HEAVENLY DOCTRINE

When Father Fernandez, one of the companions of St. Francis Xavier, was preaching the Gospel to an assembled crowd in a certain city in the Indies, one of the rabble came near him as if to speak to him, and deliberately spat in his face. The holy missioner, without saying a word or manifesting the least emotion, took out his handkerchief, wiped his face and then continued his discourse as if nothing had happened. The people were filled with astonishment at his meekness, and those who had at first laughed at the insult offered him, could not help admiring the patience with which he had received it. Among those who were present was a certain learned doctor, who, reflecting on what he had seen with his own eyes, said to himself, "Surely this stranger must be right in saying that the doctrine which he announces is a heavenly doctrine, for a law which inspires such courage and greatness of soul, and which enables its disciples to gain such a complete victory over themselves, can only come from heaven." The sermon ended, he acknowledged publicly that the virtue of the preacher had convinced him; he then asked for Baptism, which was administered with all possible solemnity. This illustrious conversion was followed by many others, a convincing proof that "Example is the best sermon."

CALUMNY NOBLY ENDURED AND INNOCENCE VINDICATED

While St. Vincent de Paul was on one occasion upon a visit to Paris, he happened to lodge in the same house and apartment with a certain magistrate, who was a native of the same province as himself. One morning when St. Vincent was sick in bed, his friend went out, leaving a large sum of money in a cupboard which he had forgotten to lock. Upon his return he found the money gone, and blinded by passion, he immediately accused St. Vincent of the theft. The Saint answered calmly, that he had not taken it, nor had he seen any one else do so. The magistrate stormed and raged, insisted on St. Vincent making up the loss, and at length drove him from the house, proclaiming him everywhere as a thief and impostor. He even went so far as to accuse him of the robbery in presence of a distinguished assembly of ecclesiastics. St. Vincent endured this public insult in silence, and contented himself with saying, "God knows the truth."

At length, after the space of six years, the real culprit was taken up for another crime in a distant part of the country, and, by the disposal of Divine Providence, was brought before the very magistrate whom he had robbed in Paris. He then confessed, that being employed by a druggist to carry some medicine to St. Vincent, he had, when the latter was not looking, abstracted the purse from the cupboard. He added that his knowledge that the crime was laid to the charge of the Saint had always caused him the most bitter remorse, and that he acknowledged the Justice of God, which had at length overtaken him. Great too was the remorse of the magistrate at the thought of what St. Vincent had had to endure from his unjust suspicions; nor did he lose a moment in writing to him to acknowledge his fault, and humbly implore his forgiveness.

St. Vincent, in relating this incident for the instruction of his young ecclesiastics, concluded in these words, "Let us, my dear brethren, judge ourselves deserving of all the evil that can be said against us, and leave to God the task of manifesting the secrets of hearts."

ST. TERESA AND THE DIVINE CHILD

St. Teresa was so inflamed with love at the thought of our Blessed Lord's goodness in becoming man and dying for her, that she looked upon this life as a continued martyrdom, through her ardent desire of being united to her Divine Spouse. It was her custom to sign all her letters, Teresa of Jesus, to show that she lived for Jesus alone, and loved him alone. One day, when she was walking through the cloisters of her convent at Avila, she met a beautiful child, who stopped when he saw her, and looked up to her face with an engaging smile. The holy nun, wondering how he had been able to enter the convent, asked him to tell her his name. "I will, if you will tell me your own," said the child. "Mine?" said St. Teresa, smiling; "I am called Teresa of Jesus." "And if you would know mine," said the child, "I am called Jesus of Teresa." At the same moment he disappeared, leaving St. Teresa's heart overflowing with wonder and gratitude at the Infinite Goodness of our Lord, who returns so tenderly the love of his unworthy creatures.

ST. EDMUND AND THE CHILD JESUS

While St. Edmund, afterwards Archbishop of Canterbury, was pursuing his studies at Paris, he would frequently walk in the fields by the river side, in order to meditate on sacred subjects. One day he beheld before him a boy of exceeding beauty, whose countenance was white and ruddy, and who saluted him, saying, "Hail, my beloved!" The stranger then asked Edmund if he did not know him. Edmund replied that he did not remember to have seen him. Upon which the boy exclaimed, "It is strange that you do not know me, for I sit by your side in the schools, and wherever you go, I am with you." He then told Edmund to look at his face and see what was written on his forehead. Edmund looked and read, "Jesus of Nazareth, King of the Jews." From that time the holy youth became more and more inflamed with the love of his Redeemer, and devoted himself more than ever to the meditation of his Sacred Passion.

ST. IGNATIUS AND THE CARRIER

It is related in the life of St. Ignatius that, being at one time on a journey with some of his pious companions, they hired a peasant to carry their baggage, for they were travelling on foot. Their carrier proved to be a very ignorant and also a very impatient and passionate man; and, when the good priests first hired him, he was much addicted to cursing and swearing, so that they frequently had occasion to reprove and exhort him. Whenever these holy men arrived at an inn, the first thing they did, after hiring a room for themselves and the carrier, was to retire into a corner and pray. In the meantime, the carrier generally slept on a bench or sat warming himself by the fire. After some time, however, observing the heavenly countenances of these holy men while thus employed, and beginning to think that it might be because they prayed so devoutly that they were so good to every one and so happy and cheerful in the midst of difficulties and privations, he determined to do as they did, and, kneeling down at a distance from them, he remained in that posture till they rose up to pursue their journey. Having continued this practice for some time, the carrier seemed to every one to be changed into another man, for he became sober, civil, patient, and obliging. The good religious with reason attributed this happy change to the help which he must have obtained from God since he applied himself to prayer; but, wishing to satisfy themselves further, they one day asked him what prayers he said. "You know that I cannot read," replied the carrier, "neither have I been taught how to pray; but this is what I say to God when I see you praying: 'Lord, I am a poor ignorant man, and I know not how to serve you; but what these holy men are doing, I at least desire to do.'" The good missionaries were much edified by the reply of the peasant, and returned thanks to God, to whom a hearty, good will is more acceptable than the finest language.

QUEEN BLANCHE AND ST. LOUIS

Queen Blanche, the mother of St. Louis, King of France, brought up her son in the most tender sentiments of piety, and in the most happy innocence. Above all things, she strove to impress upon his soul the most lively horror of sin, and a particular love of holy purity. Often, when he was a child, did she take him to her knee, and address him in these touching words, which became deeply imprinted on his heart: "I love you, my darling son, with all the tenderness of which a mother is capable, but I would rather see you dead at my feet than that you should ever commit a mortal sin." In after life, St. Louis was heard to say that not a day had passed in which these words had not been present to his mind, and helped to preserve him from sin.

HEROIC FORTITUDE OF A RECENT MARTYR

Among the numerous confessors of the Faith who, during this present century have courageously undergone torments and death in the kingdom of Tong-quin, the name of Michael Mi is deserving of special mention. He was arrested, along with his aged father-in-law, Anthony, on the charge of being concerned in the concealment of a priest, who was taken, and who suffered with them. The poor old Anthony, who was on the verge of seventy, shuddered at the sight of the instruments of torture which were displayed before the tribunal, but Michael encouraged him by reminding him of the eternal reward which they were about to purchase so cheaply, at the price of a few short and passing sufferings. "And as to the stripes which you dread, fear not, father," said he; "I will offer myself to endure them in your place." Accordingly, after he himself had been flogged without mercy, so that his whole body was a mass of wounds and blood, he, of his own accord, lay down again upon the ground, saying to the Judge, "My father is aged and infirm; take pity on him, and suffer me to be flogged in his stead." And when this was permitted, he with the greatest joy endured a second scourging, nor did a groan or sigh escape him while his wounds were being reopened, and his flesh again torn and rent asunder.

After many examinations and cruel torments, the three confessors of the Faith were at length condemned to be beheaded, and set out with serene and joyful countenances for the place of execution. Michael Mi distinguished himself especially by his undaunted courage. "Give me some money," said the executioner to him, "and I will promise to cut off your head at a single blow, so that you may have less to suffer." "Cut it into a hundred pieces if you like," said the Christian hero; "it matters not, provided that you manage somehow to cut it off. As for money, I have plenty at home, but I would rather that it should be given to the poor." So saying, he bent his head to receive the fatal strike, and went to receive the triple crown of faith, charity and filial piety.

FILIAL CONDUCT OF SIR THOMAS MORE

The great Sir Thomas More, Lord High Chancellor of England, was remarkable during his youth for his affectionate and dutiful conduct towards his parents. When he had grown up to manhood, and had been raised to the highest dignities of the State by King Henry VIII, he continued to display the same deference and respect towards his aged father, of which he had been so admirable a model when a boy. It is related of him that each morning before taking his seat in the Chancellor's Court, he was wont to repair, clad in his robes of office, to the Court of Queen's Bench. There his father, who was then far advanced in years, sat as one of the inferior judges; but though superior both in rank and office, the Lord High Chancellor of England was seen each day to come and kneel at the old man's feet to ask his blessing. So admirable an exercise of humility and filial piety drew upon him the choicest blessings of heaven. When Henry soon after threw off his obedience to the Holy See, and impiously declared himself head of the Church in England, Sir Thomas More firmly resisted every effort which the king made to draw him into his schism, and by his fidelity to the faith merited the glorious crown of martyrdom.

THE UNDUTIFUL SON

A gentleman of property had an only son whom he loved tenderly. Upon his son's marriage he gave up all he had to him on condition that he would afford him a home for the rest of his life. The old man soon became infirm, but instead of bearing patiently with the infirmities which often accompany old age, his daughter-in-law expressed herself highly disgusted with him for his want of cleanliness at his meals. One day, when they were to have company, she went so far as to tell her husband that she would not sit down to table unless the old man was made to take his dinner in the kitchen.

Her husband was so weak and unmindful of what was due to his aged parent as to consent to this heartless proposal, and accordingly bade his father go for that day to dine with the servants. The old man was cut to the quick at his son's unfilial conduct; he wept bitterly, and declared that he would sooner go and beg his bread than remain any longer with such undutiful children. His little grandson hearing what he said, and seeing him go upstairs to fetch a blanket to put over his shoulders, for it was in the depth of winter, ran to his father and told him that grandpapa was gone to get a blanket to wrap himself in that he might go and beg his bread. "Let him go, if he likes," replied the unfeeling son. "But don't let him take a whole blanket," said the child. "And why so?" asked his father. "Because I shall want the other half for you," replied the boy, "when you grow old and I turn you out to beg your bread." These words went to the heart of the father, and fearing that his undutiful conduct might one day be imitated by his own son, he ran after the old man, humbly begged his pardon, and ever after treated him with proper respect and affection.

THE ANGEL AND THE HERMIT

A certain hermit who had retired into the desert to do penance for his sins, was in the habit of going every day to a well at some distance in order to fetch water for his use. The journey was tiresome, but he made it cheerfully with the intention of pleasing God, and he usually said his prayers as he went along.

One very hot day, as he was carrying his can full of water under a broiling sun, the devil suggested to him that it was a very foolish thing to go daily such a distance for the water, when he might, if he pleased, build himself a cell close to the spring. This thought took such possession of his mind that he said to himself, "I declare I will set about it this very day, and not toil and weary myself any longer to no purpose."

While thus speaking, he was surprised to hear a voice behind him, saying, "One, two, three, four," as if there were some one walking after him and counting his steps. The hermit looked round in astonishment and beheld a lovely youth, clad in a brilliant robe of light, whom he knew at once to be an Angel. "Be not astonished," the stranger said, "I am your Guardian Angel, and I am counting your steps, that not one may pass unrewarded." With these words the beautiful vision disappeared, and the hermit giving thanks to God, went on his way with joyful steps, resolved to increase, rather than to lessen, the distance between his hermitage and the well.

WORK AND PRAY; PRAY AND WORK

The great St. Antony, who led a life of prayer and austerity in the desert, upon one occasion fell into a state of dejection because he could not keep his mind continually employed in holy contemplation. Our Blessed Lord thereupon comforted him by the following vision. Before him he beheld the figure of a hermit like himself, busily employed in platting mats out of the leaves of the palm tree. After a time, he rose from his work and began to pray. His prayer finished, he again sat down to work, but after working for a time he returned to prayer. Meanwhile he heard a voice which said,

"Work and pray; pray and work, and so thou shalt be saved."

ST. ANDREW THE APOSTLE

St. Andrew, the elder brother of St. Peter, and the first of the Apostles whom Christ called, followed his Divine Master to heaven by the same royal way of the cross. It is related that when he was led out to be crucified, as soon as he perceived at a distance the cross on which he was to suffer, he cried out, in a transport of love, "Hail, precious cross, that hast been consecrated by the Body of my Lord, and adorned with his Limbs as with rich jewels! I come to thee exulting and glad; receive me with joy into thy arms. O good cross, that hast received beauty from our Lord's Limbs, I have ardently loved thee; long have I desired and sought thee; now thou art found by me, and art made ready for my longing soul. Receive me into thy arms, taking me from among men, and present me to my Master, that he, who redeemed me on thee, may receive me by thee." So saying, he gave up his body to the executioners, and finished his holy life by a glorious death.

TRIALS OF ST. PERPETUA

During the persecution which raged against the Christian religion under the reign of the Emperor Severus, a lady of quality, named Perpetua, with an infant at her breast, was arrested with many others, and cast into a loathsome prison. Among other trials which she had to undergo, the babe that she was nursing was torn from her arms at an age when it most needed its mother's tender care; but though her heart was wrung with anguish, she generously made the sacrifice which God required from her, and committed it with confidence to the keeping of its Heavenly Father.

But the greatest of all the trials which she had to bear was at the hands of her own father, who was still a pagan, and who loved her passionately. Being admitted to have access to his daughter, in order that his entreaties and the sight of his distress might overcome her constancy, he left nothing undone to try to shake her resolution. At one time he would show her his grey hairs and the arms in which he had often carried her; at another he would throw himself at her feet and, embracing her tenderly, implore her to have compassion on him, and not to hasten his death by sacrificing her own life for her religion. The affectionate heart of Perpetua was deeply moved at the sight of the tears and distress of her aged father; but her pain was redoubled when she beheld him beaten with a stick, by order of the judge, in order to drive him from her presence. Her constancy, however, and her fidelity to Jesus Christ continued unshaken; for she remembered the Words of our Blessed Lord, "*He that loveth father or mother more than me is not worthy of me.*" (Matthew 10:37)

St. Perpetua having thus, by the power of Divine love, triumphed over the feelings of nature, completed her glorious course in the amphitheatre, where she was first tossed by a furious bull, and afterwards beheaded.

LORD, WHERE ART THOU GOING?

The little chapel of the *Domine quo vadis*, or "Lord where art thou going?" is situated on one of the roads that lead out of the city of Rome, and brings to the mind of the traveller a beautiful incident that took place on that very spot eighteen hundred years ago.

It is related in the life of St. Peter, the Prince of the Apostles, that the Emperor Nero, having raised a cruel persecution against the Church, the Christians of Rome earnestly entreated St. Peter to withdraw from the city for a while, that he might preserve a life so valuable to the whole Church. The Apostle, though unwilling, yielded to their entreaties, and under the darkness of night made his escape through the Appian gate, and turned his back on Rome. He had not proceeded far, when he met our Blessed Lord bearing his cross, and toiling painfully under the weight of it, on his road towards the city. St. Peter, thunderstruck at what he saw, exclaimed, "Lord, where art thou going?" On which our Saviour, casting upon him a look of gentle reproach, replied, "I am going to Rome to be crucified again." St. Peter at once understood that it was the Will of God that he should return to Rome and there suffer; he accordingly re-passed the gate and re-entered the city. Soon after, he was apprehended and confined in the Mamertine prison, along with St. Paul. Being condemned to be crucified, and led to execution, he begged as a special favour that he might be crucified with his head downwards, saying that he did not think himself worthy to suffer in the same manner as his Divine Master. His request was granted, and thus he added to the glory of martyrdom the crown of humility.

FINDING OF THE TRUE CROSS

When Constantine the Great had, by his miraculous victory over the Pagan Emperor Maxentius, put a stop to the long persecution, and established the Christian religion throughout his dominions, his pious mother, St. Helen, though then eighty years of age, undertook a journey to Palestine to satisfy her devotion by visiting the Holy Places. Being arrived at Jerusalem, she was filled with a longing desire of finding the very cross on which our Blessed Lord had suffered and died. On consulting the oldest of the inhabitants, she was informed that if she could only find the place of our Lord's Burial, she would be sure to find his cross at a little distance, as it was the custom among the Jews to bury the instruments of execution near to the body of the criminal. St. Helen accordingly caused the profane buildings in the neighbourhood to be cleared away, especially a temple of Venus, which the pagans had built over the very spot where our Blessed Lord had been buried. Then, digging to a great depth, she found not only the tomb, but likewise three crosses, with the nails and other instruments of the Passion.

It was now plain that one of these three crosses was that on which Jesus had died, and that the other two were the crosses of the two thieves. But how were they to distinguish the one of which they were in search? In this difficulty the holy Bishop Macarius, knowing that one of the principal ladies of the city lay extremely ill, suggested to the Empress that the three crosses should be carried in solemn procession to the sick person, not doubting that God would discover by a miracle which was the cross on which his Divine Son had died for our Redemption. This being done, St. Macarius, after earnest prayer, applied the crosses singly to the sick lady, who at the touch of the third was restored to perfect health. St. Helen, filled with joy, built a magnificent church over the spot where she had discovered the sacred relic, and there placed part of the precious wood, enclosed in a costly case. The remainder she carried to Europe, and deposited a portion of it at Rome, in the Church of the Holy Cross, which she built to receive it, and where it remains to the present day.

TRIUMPH OF THE CROSS

After the cruel persecution of the Christians by the Roman Emperors had lasted for nearly 300 years, Almighty God sent peace to his Church by the miraculous victory of Constantine over the pagan Emperor Maxentius. On the day before the battle there appeared in the sky, in sight of Constantine and the whole army, a brilliant cross of light, with this inscription, "In this thou shalt conquer." The following night our Blessed Lord appeared to Constantine in his sleep, with the same sign, and ordered him to make a copy of it, and use it as his standard in the coming battle. Constantine rose early, ordered the standard to be constructed, and caused the sacred sign of the cross to be engraved on his own helmet and the shields of his soldiers. He then marched out to battle, and gained a complete victory. On the same day he entered Rome in triumph, but instead of going to offer sacrifice to the false gods of his ancestors, he published everywhere the vision which he had beheld, and declared that his splendid victory was due only to the God of the Christians. In gratitude for this favour, he not only put a stop to the bloody persecution, which had been raging for so many years, but ordered the worship of idols to be abolished, and the Christian religion to be followed throughout his dominions. His own conversion, which took place at the same time, was soon followed by that of the greater portion of his subjects.

CONVERSION OF ST. IGNATIUS LOYOLA

The great St. Ignatius, founder of the Society of Jesus, was born of a noble family, and followed in his youth the profession of arms in the service of the king of Spain. The character of Ignatius was open, generous, and courageous; he was, however, vain of his personal appearance, fond of pleasure, and full of worldly and ambitious thoughts. He ardently longed to distinguish himself in the service of his king, and to gain for himself the esteem and applause of the world. An opportunity soon occurred to put his courage to the test. The city of Pampeluna was besieged by the French army, and, owing to the death of his superior officer, it fell to the lot of Ignatius to direct the defense. On this occasion he gave proof of great and noble qualities. Though at the head of but a small force, he scorned every proposal to surrender, encouraged the drooping spirits of the soldiers, and led them in person to attack the besiegers. In the engagement he was wounded by a cannon ball, which shattered his leg, and he was carried back helpless to the fortress.

After the surrender of the city Ignatius was permitted to retire to his own home, the Castle of Loyola, where he remained for many months helpless and confined to his bed. To while away the time, he desired his attendants to bring him some romances or tales of chivalry, but they could find no such books in the castle. They brought him, however, a volume of the Lives of the Saints, which they had met with in their search. Ignatius at first laid it impatiently aside, as ill suited to his taste; but seeing that no other book could be procured, he at length opened and began to read it. By degrees his attention became awakened, and he could not help admiring the noble generosity of men who had sacrificed fortune, worldly honour, and even life itself in the service of God. He soon began to compare their lives with his own, to reflect on the emptiness and vanity of all that passes with time, and to understand how wisely the Saints had acted in preferring the service of the King of Heaven to that of an earthly monarch. From that time Ignatius resolved to occupy himself no longer with the vain pursuit of earthly glory, but to devote himself to the great work of obtaining the victory over his own passions and promoting the glory of his Heavenly Master. Accordingly upon his recovery he retired into solitude, where he gave himself up to the practice of penance and prayer. Soon after he laid the foundation of the illustrious order of the Jesuits, the members of which, by the great works which they have performed for the education of youth and the preaching of the Gospel, have so well fulfilled those words which St. Ignatius took as the rule and motto of his life: *Ad majorem Dei Gloriam* — "All to the greater Glory of God."

ST. AUGUSTINE'S EXPERIENCE OF THE USE OF GOOD BOOKS

A certain courtier, a friend of St. Augustine, was one day walking near the city of Triers with three of his gay companions, when two of them, who were officers in the Emperor's army, chanced to enter a cottage which was the dwelling-place of some devout servants of God. Here they perceived upon the table a copy of the life of the great St. Anthony the hermit, which one of them opened through curiosity. Attracted, says St. Augustine, by something which caught his eye, he began to read, and reading, to admire, and admiring, to burn with the desire of imitating so noble and heroic an example. At length inflamed with what he read, and burning with a holy zeal, he cried out to his companion, "Tell me, I pray, with all the pains we take, what does our ambition aspire to? Have we any greater hopes at court than to arrive at the friendship and favour of the Emperor? And when this is obtained, how long will it last? But behold, if I please, I can become this moment the friend and favourite of God, and remain so for ever." So saying, he paused; but having read a little further, he again exclaimed, "Behold, now I bid adieu to former hopes, and am fully resolved to have no other pursuit but that of serving God. I begin from this very hour, in this very place. As for you, if you do not imitate my example, at least do not hinder my resolution." The other replied that, so far from hindering him, he wished to stand by his side in so noble a warfare. Accordingly, taking leave of their companions, they remained in the cottage; upon receiving news of which, the two young ladies to whom they were engaged, consecrated their virginity to God.

This example, which was related to St. Augustine by his friend Pontitianus, at a time when his mind was still wavering between the force of truth and the violence of his passions, raised immediately a mighty conflict within his breast. Agitated by his feelings, and drawn by the grace of God, he retired into the garden to pray. Here he poured forth the anguish of his heart with bitter sighs and tears, when suddenly he heard the voice of a child frequently repeating these words, "*Tolle lege; tolle lege;*—take and read; take and read." Upon this, rising up in amazement, he went to fetch the book of St. Paul's Epistles, which he had left hard by, and opening it, he lighted upon the words, "*Put ye on the Lord Jesus Christ, and make no provision for the flesh and its concupiscences.*" He read no further, nor had he need; for at the end of these lines a new gleam of confidence and security streamed into his heart, and all the darkness of his former hesitation was dispelled. He immediately went in and told the good news to his mother, St. Monica, who was transported with joy. He then put himself under the care of St. Ambrose, who shortly after conferred upon him the sacrament of Baptism.

THE IRISH SERVANT GIRL

A few years ago there lived in London a gentleman who was extremely prejudiced against our holy religion, and never lost an opportunity of laughing at and ridiculing its practices. Upon one occasion, however, when Catholic doctrines became the subject of conversation and ridicule, it was noticed that he preserved a grave silence. Being asked the reason, he related to the company the following story:

"You wonder," said he, "why I no longer join with you, as I used to do, in scoffing at Catholic practices; I will tell you. A few days ago I was busy writing in my room, when I had occasion to leave my desk in order to fetch a certain paper from an inner apartment. While I was so engaged, the servant girl, who is an Irish Catholic, happened to enter the room to mend the fire, for, as I had not answered to her knock, she imagined that I had gone out. Now, I had left by chance upon my desk a large sum of money, and I could see that, as soon as she entered the room, she was attracted by the glitter of the gold. I determined to watch her narrowly, for I was in a position to observe all her movements, though she had no knowledge of my presence. On perceiving the gold she dropped the coal-box, and advanced eagerly to the table. She then stretched out her hand, and was on the very point of clutching the money, when, to my astonishment, she suddenly withdrew her arm and made with her hand the sign of the cross, saying aloud, 'The Cross of Christ be betwixt me and my master's money!' She then turned her back and fairly ran out of the room, leaving her brush and coal-box on the floor. "Now I am convinced from this that the pious practices of the Catholic religion, so far from being idle and superstitious, are most holy and pleasing to God, since they are the means of raising the heart to him, and drawing down grace in moments of strong temptation."

DANIEL AND HIS YOUNG COMPANIONS

Nabuchodonosor, king of Babylon, having taken and plundered Jerusalem, and carried into captivity the remnant of the Jewish race, instructed his chief eunuch Asphenez to select from among the conquered people certain youths, distinguished alike for birth, comeliness and talent, who might abide in the king's palace and learn the language and customs of the Chaldeans. "And the king appointed them," relates the prophet Daniel, "a daily provision of his own meat and of the wine of which he drank himself, that, being nourished three years, afterwards they might stand before the king."

"Now there were of the children of Juda: Daniel, Ananias, Misael, and Azarias. But Daniel purposed in his heart that he would not be defiled with the king's table, nor with the wine which he drank, and he requested the master of the eunuchs that he might not be defiled. And God gave to Daniel grace and mercy in the sight of the prince of the eunuchs. And the prince of the eunuchs said to Daniel, 'I fear my lord the king, who hath appointed you meat and drink; who, if he should see your face leaner than those of the other youths your equals, you shall endanger my head to the king.' And Daniel said to Malasar, whom the prince of the eunuchs had appointed over Daniel, Ananias, Misael, and Azarias, 'Try, I beseech thee, thy servants for ten days, and let pulse be given us to eat and water to drink. And look upon our faces and the faces of the children who eat of the king's meat, and as thou shalt see, deal with thy servants.' And when he had heard these words he tried them for ten days; and after the ten days their faces appeared fairer and fatter than all the children that eat of the king's meat. And when the days were ended after which the king had ordered they should be brought in, the prince of the eunuchs brought them in before Nabuchodonosor. And when the king had spoken to them, there were not found among them all such as Daniel, Ananias, Misael and Azarias, and they stood in the king's presence. And in all matters of wisdom and understanding that the king inquired of them, he found them ten times better than all the diviners and wise men that were in all his kingdom."

ANECDOTES OF LOUIS XVI

It is related of the unfortunate Louis XVI, king of France, who died on the scaffold during the great French revolution, that when he was a youth of twenty years he said one day to his courtiers, "I have not done much in the way of keeping Lent this year, but next year it will be different, for I shall have to fast." "Sire," said one of them, "that will be impossible, for you would not be able to hunt." "No matter," replied Louis, "I must give up hunting if it is necessary, for a mere amusement does not excuse any one from obeying the laws of the Church."

Among other abuses which the young king abolished on coming to the throne of France, was that of serving up both fish and meat at the royal table on the great hunting days when they happened also to be days of abstinence. A certain officer grumbled at the new regulation, quoting the words of our Blessed Lord, *"Not that which goeth into the mouth defileth a man."* (Mt. 15:11) "You are right," replied the king, "it is not the meat we eat which injures the body, but the disobedience we are guilty of that kills the soul. Whosoever will not hear the Church, says our Lord, let him be to thee as the heathen and the publican. (Mt. 18:17) Now, I do not think you would like to be called either one or the other."

The same king, when in prison and in the hands of his merciless enemies, was equally exact in observing the days of abstinence, and was wont to content himself for his meal with a piece of dry bread, when forbidden food was placed before him in derision by his cruel jailer.

TRUE OBEDIENCE

In one of the principal cities of France there lived a young boy, whose parents were so neglectful of the practice of their religion that they used flesh meat on all days alike, without regard to the laws of the Church. When he was being prepared for his first Communion the boy went to confession, and among his other faults accused himself of not keeping the days of abstinence. His confessor explained to him the greatness of the sin of which he had had hitherto little or no idea, and laid down rules for his conduct in future which he promised faithfully to observe.

It was not long before his resolution was put to the test, for on the following Friday nothing was served up for dinner but the usual forbidden fare. The young boy was helped like the rest, but begged to be excused from taking it. His father was much astonished, and immediately demanded the cause of his refusal. He replied that it was an abstinence day, on which it was forbidden by the Church to eat flesh meat, adding that he was quite ready to make his dinner on the bread and vegetables. His father, enraged at his resolution, took him from the table without allowing him to eat a mouthful, and shut him up in a solitary room, telling him that he should remain there until the following day. The boy made no answer, and submitted to his punishment without a murmur.

In the course of the same evening his mother who, though as negligent about the duties of her religion as her husband, could not help feeling for the privations of her child, came to see him and brought him some food, at the same time reproving him for his obstinacy and disobedience. What was her surprise when he refused to partake of it! "My father," said he, "has condemned me to fast till tomorrow, and as I can obey him in that without sin I would rather not eat what you have been so good as to bring me." The mother, much affected at hearing her child express himself with such sense and modesty, left the room, and went to tell her husband what had passed. The latter was equally struck with the admirable conduct of his child, and agreed with his wife that the boy was much more reasonable than themselves. He at once went to his room, tenderly embraced him, and asked him who had taught him to be so faithful to his duty. Learning that it was his confessor, the father went to visit him without delay, thanked him for the care he had taken of his son, and begged of him to hear his own confession. His conversion was sincere, and was soon followed by that of his wife. The noble conduct of the child was thus the happy means of reconciling his parents to Almighty God.

THE COUNTRYMAN AND THE VIPERS

A countryman walking one day through the woods, fell in with a nest of vipers. At first sight of them he was afraid and started back, but at length summoning up courage, he returned and took the nest, which contained a brood of seven young vipers. For three weeks he kept this singular family in his house, feeding them meanwhile with bread and milk, till one day a friend came to see him. "You should not forget," said the visitor, "that if you do not destroy these vipers now while they are young, but on the contrary go on feeding them, they will grow very quickly, and you may depend upon it that sooner or later they will fasten on you with their poisonous fangs, and you will fall a victim to your imprudence." "Oh, never fear," said the countryman, "they are only young, and I have plenty of time before me. Besides, I take great precaution, and if ever I find them dangerous I can soon get rid of them." "Do not rely upon that," said his friend, "for in all probability they will take you by surprise." To this the owner of the vipers made no answer, and his friend took his leave, but not without feeling serious uneasiness. A few days after, he returned, and found the countryman in dreadful torture, for he had just been bitten by the dangerous reptiles. His friend hastened to his assistance, but it was too late, the poison had entered his blood, and he soon after expired.

THE HERMIT AND HIS DISCIPLE

A certain hermit who dwelt in a cave in the deserts of Thebaïs, had a virtuous disciple whom he was in the habit of instructing each evening, after which he was accustomed to dismiss him to bed with his blessing. One night it happened that the hermit fell asleep while giving his instruction, and slept so soundly that he did not awake till after midnight. The young man waited in vain for the hermit to awake, that they might make their usual evening prayer together, and that he might retire to rest. At length he grew very drowsy, and was strongly tempted to leave his master and go to bed, but he resisted the temptation and continued to watch by his side. Seven times was he tempted in the same manner, for his eyes were heavy, and he was very weary with watching, but still he persevered, for he was determined that sloth should not prevail over him. At length his master awoke, and finding his disciple by his side, asked him why he had not retired to rest. "Because," replied the youth, "you did not dismiss me." "But why did you not awake me?" said the hermit. "Father," replied his disciple, "I could not presume to disturb you." Thereupon they said their prayers, and the hermit dismissed him to bed. Then falling into an ecstasy, the old man beheld a magnificent palace, in which was placed a throne, and over it seven crowns of glory. At the same time he was told by an Angel, that they were destined to reward his diligent disciple, who had that night merited these seven crowns, by his generous resistance to the temptations of Satan.

THE HERMIT'S ANSWER TO HIS DISCIPLES

A certain hermit, being one day asked by his disciples in what manner they could best secure the victory over their passions, took them into a plantation of cypress trees, which were of different sizes, according to the length of time which they had been planted. Pointing to a very little one, he bade one of his disciples pull it up, which he did very easily with one hand, for it was only a few days since it had been placed in the ground. He then pointed to another somewhat bigger, which his disciple also pulled up, but he had to take both hands to it, and to exert his strength, for having been planted a few months, its roots had already begun to take hold of the soil. A third, which had been a year in the ground, the youth found himself quite unable to uproot; so his companions came to help him, and by their united strength they at length succeeded in extracting it. The hermit then pointed to a fourth, of some years' growth, but all their efforts to pull it out of the ground produced not the slightest effect. Upon which the hermit said, "My children, so it is with our passions. When they are yet young and have not taken root, it is easy with a little care to overcome them; but when by long habit they have become rooted in our souls, it is very difficult indeed to subdue them. Strive, then, now while you are young, to destroy these enemies, who otherwise will cause you severe conflicts when you grow older, and may even be the cause of your eternal ruin."

CONVERSION OF THE BULGARIANS

The Bulgarians, a people dwelling on the banks of the Danube, remained till the ninth century buried in idolatry. About that time it happened that the sister of the King, Boigoris, was taken prisoner by the Emperor of Constantinople, and during her captivity was converted to the Christian faith. On her return to her own country she tried to convince her brother of the folly of idolatry and the beauty and excellence of the Christian religion; but Boigoris, though he admitted the truth of all she said, remained obstinate in the worship of his false gods.

Now it happened that the King, who was engaged in decorating his palace, sent to Constantinople for an artist, hoping to obtain from thence one of greater merit than could be found in his own country. The Emperor sent him a monk, named Methodius, who was remarkable for his skill in painting. Boigoris immediately set him to work, bidding him paint on the walls of the gallery some picture of so terrible a nature that it should strike fear into all who beheld it. The good monk promised to do so, and, while he was at work, caused a curtain to be extended before that portion of the wall which he was decorating, so that the picture might not be seen by any one until it was completed.

When the work was finished, and the day arrived for removing the curtain, the King and all his court assembled to witness the result. The curtain was withdrawn, and the King beheld before his eyes a faithful representation of the last judgment; for Methodius, thinking no scene so terrible as this, had chosen it for his subject. He had represented in lively colours kings, princes, and people standing before the throne of the Great Judge, who appeared armed with all the terrors of Majesty and Justice, and attended by ministering angels. Other angels were represented as separating the good from the bad, and placing some on the right and some on the left hand of Almighty God.

The King was struck with terror at the sight, and listened eagerly while the holy monk explained to him the different portions of the picture, exhorting him at the same time to take such steps now as would secure for himself a place among the Saints of God when that great day should at length arrive.

The instructions of Methodius, assisted by the grace of God, were not without effect. Boigoris was shortly after baptized, and his conversion was soon followed by that of the whole nation.

THE INDIAN CACIQUE

Soon after the discovery and invasion of North America by the Spaniards, an Indian chieftain or *Cacique* was brought before the Spanish Governor, charged with conspiracy and attempt to revolt. The Governor sat in his chair of state, surrounded by his officers, and with his naked sword suspended from his belt. The poor Indian stood before him unarmed, half naked, and loaded with fetters. When the charge had been read, the Governor, turning to the Cacique, asked him what he had to say in his defense. The poor Indian, having in vain protested his innocence, at length advancing to the Governor's feet, and taking hold, with his fettered hand, of the glittering steel, said, in tones of true sincerity, "Judge for yourself, Governor, whether it is likely that I should be so mad as to revolt against one who bears a weapon like this."

THE BUNCH OF GRAPES

It is related in the life of St. Macarius, one of the Fathers of the Desert, that he one day received a present of a beautiful bunch of grapes. Though he felt a longing desire to taste the fruit, he determined to deny himself, and in order to exercise himself at the same time in mortification and charity, he sent them on to another hermit, who lived at a little distance, and whom he knew to be sick and infirm. The sick man, however, was inspired with the same thought as St. Macarius, and sent them on to a third hermit, and he to a fourth, until in this manner they had travelled through most of the cells in the desert without any one tasting a single grape. In the end it happened that the hermit who received them last, not knowing whence they had come, sent them as a present to the holy Abbot St. Macarius. The Saint perceiving them to be the very same grapes which had been first offered to him, and learning on inquiry through whose hands they had passed, returned thanks to God for the great spirit of self-denial which the brethren had shown. Nevertheless, it is recorded that he could not himself be induced to taste of the grapes.

THE FIREMAN'S DAUGHTER

A large number of children were assembled at their lessons in a public schoolroom a few years since, when suddenly an alarm was given that the house was on fire. The children ran here and there in the greatest terror, seeking everywhere for the means of escape, and one of the pupil teachers was so terrified that she threw herself from the window of the room, which was on the second story, into the street below. In the midst of the general alarm, it was remarked that one of the little girls never attempted to escape, and though excessively pale and trembling, never stirred from the form where she was seated. When the alarm was discovered to be unfounded and order was restored, the schoolmistress asked the little girl how it was that she had sat so still the whole time, while every one else had been trying to escape. "Please, ma'am" said she, "it's because father is a fireman, and has often told me, if ever there was an alarm of fire, to sit quite still."

DEATH RATHER THAN A LIE

During the great French Revolution, at the end of last century, the Catholic churches were pillaged throughout the country, and closed for public worship. The priests also were proscribed, and forced to conceal themselves in private houses, or even to seek shelter in the thickets of the forests or in the caves and fastnesses of the mountains. It happened about this time that a young girl, named Magdalen Larralde, of the village of Sare, on the borders of Spain, fearing to have recourse to her own parish priest in his place of concealment, was wont to cross the mountains whenever she desired to approach the Sacraments, in order to seek spiritual assistance from the Capuchin Fathers at Vera, on the Spanish side of the Pyrenees. One day, on returning from the convent, she fell in with an outpost of the French army, which was then stationed along the frontier, in consequence of the war which raged between the two countries. The soldiers immediately seized her as a spy, and dragged her before the general, who questioned her as to the object of her presence in Spain. Magdalen answered simply and without a moment's hesitation that she had been to confession. The officer, touched by her youth and innocent bearing, and anxious, if possible, to save her, quickly replied, "Unfortunate woman, do not say that, for it will be your sentence of death. Say, rather, that the advance of the French troops frightened you, and drove you to seek shelter on Spanish ground." "But then I should say what would not be true," answered the girl, "and I would rather die a thousand times than offend God by telling a lie." In vain did the general urge and solicit her to yield; her firmness never gave way, and she was conducted before the tribunal at St. Jean de Luz. Before her judges,

Magdalen again, with unflinching courage, refused to save her life by a lie. She was, therefore, condemned to the guillotine, and, as she walked to the place of execution, her step never faltered, and she ceased not to invoke the assistance of God, chanting aloud the *Salve Regina* in honour of the Queen of Heaven.

THE BISHOP AND THE SOLDIERS

It is related in Church History that upon one occasion the emperor Maximinian, a cruel persecutor of the faithful, despatched a troop of soldiers to apprehend and cast into prison Antony, the venerable Bishop of Nicomedia. It happened that, without knowing it, they came to the house of the holy Bishop, and being hungry, knocked at the door and begged for some refreshment. He received them with great kindness, invited them to sit down at table, and set before them such food as he had at his disposal. When the meal was ended, the soldiers entered upon the subject of their mission, and requested him to inform them where they could meet with the Bishop Antony. "He is here before you," replied the Saint. The soldiers, full of gratitude for his generous hospitality, declared that they would never lay hands upon him, but would report to the emperor that they had not been able to find him. "God forbid," replied the Saint, "that I should save my life by becoming a party to a lie. I would rather die a thousand times than that you should offend Almighty God." So saying, he gave himself into their hands, and was conducted to prison.

THE MARTYR OF CONFESSION

In the fourteenth century there lived at Prague, the capital of Bohemia, a holy priest named John, called Nepomucene from Nepomuk, the city of his birth. So great was his reputation for virtue and piety, that the Empress chose him as the director of her conscience, and under his guidance arrived at an eminent degree of sanctity. This holy woman had much to endure from the jealousy of her husband Wenceslas, a man of violent passions, who nourished the most unfounded suspicions regarding his virtuous consort. Blinded by jealousy, he formed the impious design of inducing St. John to reveal to him the confession of the Empress, and actually proposed this to him, promising in case of his compliance, to load him with riches and honours. The Saint, struck with horror at the proposal, represented freely to the Emperor the enormity of such criminal curiosity, and the impossibility of gratifying it. Wenceslas dissembled his displeasure at the time, but the holy priest judged from his gloomy silence what he was to expect from so revengeful a prince.

Shortly afterwards, St. John, having ventured to remonstrate with the Emperor on occasion of an act of brutal cruelty, was thrown by him into a dungeon, with a promise of liberty as soon as he consented to disclose the confession of the Empress. Finding his resolution unshaken, Wenceslas determined to try again the effect of flatteries and caresses. He accordingly released the Saint from prison, invited him to dine at the royal table, and lavished upon him every mark of honour and esteem. When all the guests had retired after the banquet, the Emperor earnestly besought St. John to consent to his proposal, engaging on his part to preserve an inviolable secrecy, and to bestow upon him the highest dignities and a princely fortune. On the other hand, he threatened him in case of refusal with the most cruel tortures and even with death itself. The Saint answered courageously, that he would readily lay down his life rather than betray his sacred trust. Upon this the Emperor, transported with fury, called the executioners and delivered St. John into their hands, bidding them to employ every effort to move him to submission. They accordingly carried him back to prison, and having stretched him upon the rack, applied lighted torches to the most tender parts of his body. It was all to no purpose; the only words which passed his lips under the extremity of his torments, were the sacred names of Jesus and Mary.

After a short time, the Saint was once more withdrawn from prison, and restored to liberty by the capricious Wenceslas, but feeling a conviction that his martyrdom would not be long delayed, he devoted his few remaining days to a fervent preparation for death. As he was returning one day from a pilgrimage of devotion to a neighbouring shrine of the Blessed Virgin, the Emperor happened to observe him from the windows of his palace, and burning anew with sacrilegious curiosity, summoned him into his presence, and renewed his wicked proposal. The Saint answered only by his silence, upon which Wenceslas cried out in a rage, "Take away this man from before my eyes, and throw him into the river as soon as it shall be dark, that his execution may not be known to the people." This barbarous order was carried into effect the same night, but a heavenly light appeared resting over the lifeless body of the Saint, which floated on the surface of the waters, and the whole city flocked to the banks of the river to observe the prodigy. Thus was the foul deed discovered, and the relics of the martyr rescued from the waves. The sacred remains were carried in solemn procession by the clergy to the nearest church, where they were interred with great honour, Almighty God testifying to the sanctity of his servant by numerous miracles.

ST. TERESA'S VISION OF HELL

"Our Lord was pleased that one day while in prayer, I should find myself, though I could not tell how, suddenly lodged in a place in hell. It lasted but a short space of time, but if I should live for many years I could never forget it. The entrance seemed to be a long close passage, or rather like a low dark and narrow oven. The ground seemed to be like mire, exceedingly filthy, of a horrible smell, and full of a multitude of loathsome vermin. At the end of it was a certain hollow place, like a kind of little press in a wall, into which I found myself thrust and closely pent up. Now though all that I have just said was far more terrible than I have described it, yet it might be looked upon as delightful in comparison with what I felt while I was in the press. For this torment was so dreadful, that no words can express the least part of it. I felt a kind of fire in my soul which I am not able to describe. The almost insupportable torments which I have endured by the shrinking up of my sinews and in other ways, were all nothing at all in comparison with what I suffered here, joined to the dismal thought that it was to be without end or intermission. And even this itself is little, compared with the continual agony the soul is in—that pressing, that stifling, that bitter anguish, accompanied with inexpressible disgust, so harrowing, yet so hopeless. To say it is a butchering or rendering of the soul, is to say little; here she is her own executioner, and even tears herself to pieces. I saw not who it was that tormented me, but methought I felt myself both burnt and cut in pieces all at once. And in so dreadful a place there was no room for the least hope of a possibility of ever meeting with any comfort or ease; neither was there such a thing as sitting or lying down. Thus was I thrust into this place like a hole in the wall, and these walls, which are also most terrible to the sight, press in upon their prisoner, for everything there chokes and stifles. There is nothing but gross darkness, without the least glimpse of light, and yet I know not how it is, although there is no light, yet one sees everything that can afflict the sight. Afterwards, I had another vision of terrible things, inflicted as punishments for certain vices, which as far as I could judge of them by the sight, seemed to be more hideous than the former."

"Since that time all seems easy to me, in comparison with one moment of such suffering as I endured there. In short, the torments of this world are no more than a mere picture, and the burning which is felt here, but a trifle in comparison with the fire there. I remained so astonished and amazed at it, and am so even now, though it happened six years ago, that at the very thought of it my blood seems to chill in my veins through fear. And whatever troubles or pains I now suffer, if I do but call to my remembrance what I then endured, immediately all that can be suffered in this world seems to be just nothing."

THE THREE STATIONS

We read of a certain holy man, that whenever he approached the Sacrament of Penance, he was accustomed in preparing himself to make three stations or spiritual visits, one to the damned souls in hell, another to the blessed in heaven, and the third to our Lord on Mount Calvary. In his first visit he meditated on the torments endured by the devils and the lost souls: the everlasting fire, the worm that never dies, the dark prison house whose gates are never opened, the bitter remorse of the damned, and their unavailing despair at the remembrance of so many graces and opportunities that they have abused, and of the eternal delights which they have bartered away, as Esau did his birthright, for a mess of potage, a miserable and momentary gratification. Having thus aroused himself to a horror and hatred of sin, which is the cause of so much misery, he passed on to make his second station in heaven, where he considered the eternal happiness of the just, the delights of paradise which are so far beyond all human understanding, the sweet society of the Saints and Angels, the everlasting enjoyment and possession of God. "All this," thought he, "is lost by a single mortal sin, but may be regained by a true and sincere repentance." The third station he made on Mount Calvary at the foot of the cross. There, he read in the Bleeding Wounds of our Lord the infinite malice and enormity of sin, which required nothing less than the Blood of the Son of God to cancel and atone for it. There too, he contemplated with loving gratitude the Infinite Goodness and Tender Compassion of Him, who for the love of us became as a worm and no man, the reproach of men and the outcast of the people (Ps. 21:7), who bore the weight of our sins in his own innocent flesh (1 Peter 2:24), who was wounded for our iniquities and bruised for our sins, by whose bruises we were healed (Isaias 53:5). Thus did this holy penitent in these three stations gradually raise himself from fear to hope, and from hope to love; until at length, penetrated with a deep hatred and sorrow for his past sins and a loving confidence in the Divine Goodness, he entered the confessional to lay down his burden at the feet of his merciful Saviour.

"I WEEP BECAUSE YOU DO NOT WEEP"

A certain sinner, who had been guilty of enormous crimes, made his confession one day to St. Francis of Sales, who received him with the tenderest compassion. Seeing, however, that the penitent accused himself of the most heinous sins without the least appearance of remorse or confusion, the Saint burst into tears. The sinner, far from imagining that it was his own crimes which drew tears from the heart of the Saint, asked him if he was in any pain. St. Francis replied, "I am very well, my brother, thank God; but, alas! you are far from well." The other boldly answered that nothing ailed him, and went on in the same hardened strain. Thereupon, the Saint's tears fell more freely. Again the penitent asked him why he was weeping. "Alas!" he replied, "I weep because you do not weep." At these words the sinner was touched with compunction. "Wretched man that I am," exclaimed he, "to feel no sorrow or shame for my own enormous sins, when they draw tears from one who is innocent!" So powerfully was he moved by Divine grace that he fell at the Saint's feet, shedding abundant tears, and imploring his assistance and advice. St. Francis, overjoyed at this happy conversion, now encouraged and consoled him, and having prepared him by a good act of contrition to receive the grace of absolution, had the happiness of restoring his penitent to the love and friendship of God. From that time the sinner gave himself entirely to the Divine service, and became a model of true penance.

This touching incident, says the historian of St. Francis, was related in after life by the penitent himself, who used to add, "There are many confessors who make their penitents weep, but I have drawn tears from my confessor himself."

THERE IS MERCY FOR EVERY SIN

A certain woman, who was a great sinner, was one day crossing a church, which she had entered with the sole intention of shortening her way, when she perceived a number of people crowding in, as if to assist at some public service. Moved by curiosity, she took her seat among the rest, and the crowd increasing, she soon found herself so surrounded that it was impossible to think of withdrawing. Soon after, a venerable priest entered the pulpit, and began to preach on the Goodness of God to sinners. Among other things, he several times repeated these words, "My brethren, there is mercy for every sin, provided that the sinner repents." These words touched the heart of the woman and became deeply impressed upon her mind.

No sooner was the sermon ended, than this poor sinner made her way through the crowd, and as the preacher came down from the pulpit, pulled him by the sleeve, saying to him with great simplicity, "Father, is it really true that there is pardon for every sin?" "Certainly," he replied, "God forgives all sinners, if they only repent." "But there are many kinds of sinners," she answered; "does God forgive them all, without any exception?" "Assuredly he does," replied the priest, "provided that they detest their sins." "But will he pardon me," said the woman, "who for fifteen years have been committing the most grievous crimes?" "Undoubtedly he will," replied the missioner, "if you only detest them, and give up committing them." "If that is the case, father," said the woman, "please to tell me at what hour you can hear my confession." "Immediately," said the priest, pointing to his confessional. "Kneel down there, and I will be with you directly." Accordingly, having returned from the sacristy, he heard her confession, which she made with sentiments of the deepest compunction.

Her confession being completed, the poor woman acquainted her confessor with the extreme danger to which she would be exposed were she to return to her usual place of abode to pass the night. As, however, it was impossible at that hour to procure her another shelter, he allowed her to remain in the church during the night, a permission of which she gladly availed herself. On the following morning, when the doors were opened, she was found lifeless in the chapel of the Blessed Virgin. There, prostrate on the ground, which she had watered with her tears, she had bewailed the sins of her life so sincerely, that she had expired from excess of grief—a true victim of penance, and striking example of the truth of those words, which had been the means of her conversion, "There is mercy for every sin, provided that the sinner repents."

PARABLE OF THE PRODIGAL SON

"A certain man had two sons. And the younger of them said to his father: Father, give me the portion of substance that falleth to me. And he divided unto them his substance.

"And not many days after, the younger son gathering all together, went abroad into a far country, and there wasted his substance living riotously. And after he had spent all, there came a mighty famine in that country, and he began to be in want. And he went and cleaved to one of the citizens of that country. And he sent him into his farm to feed swine. And he would fain have filled his belly with the husks the swine did eat; and no man gave unto him.

"And returning to himself, he said, How many hired servants in my father's house abound with bread and I here perish with hunger! I will arise and will go to my father, and say to him, 'Father, I have sinned against heaven and before thee. I am not now worthy to be called thy son, make me as one of thy hired servants'

"And rising up he came to his father, and when he was yet a great way off, his father saw him, and was moved with compassion, and running to him, fell upon his neck and kissed him. And the son said to him, Father, I have sinned against heaven and before thee, I am not now worthy to be called thy son. And the father said to his servants, Bring forth quickly the first robe and put it on him, and put a ring on his hand and shoes on his feet. And bring hither the fatted calf and kill it, and let us eat and make merry; because this my son was dead and is come to life again, was lost and is found. And they began to be merry.

"Now his elder son was in the field, and when he came and drew nigh to the house, he heard music and dancing; and he called one of the servants and asked what these things meant. And he said to him, Thy brother is come, and thy father hath killed the fatted calf because he hath received him safe. And he was angry and would not go in. His father, therefore, coming out began to entreat him. And he answering, said to his father, Behold, for so many years do I serve thee, and I have never transgressed thy commandment, and yet thou hast never given me a kid to make merry with my friends. But as soon as this thy son hath come, who hath devoured his substance with harlots, thou hast killed for him the fatted calf. But he said to him, Son, thou art always with me, and all I have is thine. But it was fit that we should make merry and be glad, for this thy brother was dead, and is come to life again; he was lost, and is found." —Luke 15:11-32.

NAAMAN CURED OF HIS LEPROSY

"Naaman, general of the army of the king of Syria, was a great man with his master, and he was a valiant man and rich, but a leper. Now, there had gone out robbers from Syria, and had led away captive out of the land of Israel a little maid, and she waited upon Naaman's wife. And she said to her mistress, I wish my master had been with the prophet that is in Samaria, He would certainly have healed him of the leprosy which he hath! Then Naaman went to his lord and told him. And the king of Syria said to him, Go, and I will send a letter to the king of Israel.

"And he departed, and took with him ten talents of silver and six thousand pieces of gold, and ten changes of raiment. And brought the letter to the king of Israel in these words, When thou shalt receive this letter, know that I have sent to thee Naaman my servant, that thou mayest heal him of his leprosy. And when the king of Israel had read the letter, he rent his garments and said, Am I God, to be able to kill and give life, that this man hath sent to me to heal a man of his leprosy? Mark and see, how he seeketh occasions against me. And when Eliseus, the man of God, had heard this, he sent to him saying, Why hast thou rent thy garments? Let him come to me and let him know that there is a prophet in Israel.

"So Naaman came with his horses and chariots, and stood at the door of the house of Eliseus. And Eliseus sent a messenger to him saying, Go and wash seven times in the Jordan, and thou shalt be clean. Naaman was angry, and went away, saying, I thought he would have come out to me, and standing would have invoked the name of the Lord his God, and touched with his hands the place of the leprosy, and healed me. Are not the Abana and the Pharphar, rivers of Damascus, better than all the waters of Israel, that I may wash in them and be made clean? So as he turned and was going away in indignation, his servants came to him, and said to him, Father, if the prophet had bid thee do some great thing, surely thou shouldst have done it, how much rather what he now hath said to thee, Wash and thou shalt be clean!

"Then he went down, and washed in the Jordan seven times, according to the word of the man of God, and his flesh was restored like the flesh of a little child, and he was made clean. And returning to the man of God with all his train, he said, Now I know there is no other God in all the earth but only in Israel" —4 Kings 5.

FALSE HUMILITY

A stranger monk having come to visit the holy Abbot Serapion, the latter out of respect for his visitor, begged him to give out the prayer which they were accustomed to recite on such occasions. His visitor excused himself, saying that he was a poor sinner, and unworthy to wear the religious habit. Shortly after, the Saint offered to wash his feet, according to their pious custom, but he would by no means permit him, alleging his great unworthiness. St. Serapion accordingly entertained him at table with what his cell could afford, and then dismissed him with this charitable advice: "My son, if you wish to make progress in religion, return to your cell, and there, attending to God and yourself, employ yourself in working with your hands; for coming abroad in this manner is not so good for you as it would be to remain at home." At these words signs of displeasure appeared in the face of the monk, his pride not being able to bear a rebuke. Upon which the holy Abbot said, "A little while ago you said that you were a great sinner, unworthy to wear the habit of a monk, and now you are offended at the charitable warning I have given you." At these words the monk entered into himself, and having acknowledged his fault, departed, much edified with the lesson he had received.

POWER OF PRAYER

Many years ago, in times of persecution, a Catholic Bishop, while travelling in the Highlands of Scotland, for the purpose of visiting the scattered members of his flock, was benighted one dark and stormy night in the midst of a lonely and desolate tract of country. After wandering about for some time in the greatest uncertainty, he was guided at length by the glimmering of a light to a lonely cabin, at the door of which he knocked, and begged for a night's lodging. The woman of the house received him with frank hospitality, bade him welcome to the warm fireside, and apologised for not being able to offer him a bed. "The only one that we have," said she, "is now occupied by my husband, who is lying at the point of death." "I am truly sorry to hear of your affliction," said the Bishop, "but I trust he is well prepared for so great a change." "Alas," said the woman, wiping her eyes, "he will not be persuaded that his end is so near. Though he is above eighty, and though the doctor says that his hours are numbered, yet he persists in saying that his time is not yet come." "Will you allow me to speak to him?" said the Bishop; "perhaps the opinion of a stranger may have greater weight, and he may be persuaded to prepare for his approaching departure." "Willingly," said the woman; and with that she led the way into the inner room.

Having approached the bedside, the Bishop saw that there was little time to be lost; everything betokened the near approach of death. This he did not conceal from the old man, and he exhorted him to make good use of the few hours which remained to him upon earth; but his words seemed to produce but little impression. "Sir," said the old man, "I know that my age is great. I know that my strength is almost gone. I even grant that if I saw another in the state in which I am, I would say he was at the point of death; but, for all that, I know that my time is not yet come."

"My dear friend," said the Bishop, "do not deceive yourself. Why should not death come to you as well as to the rest of men? What can have put so strange a delusion into your head?"

"I will tell you then, sir, said the old man, raising himself up in bed. "Why should I fear now what man can do to me? I am a Catholic. I have remained faithful to my God, in spite of every danger and every difficulty, though in this wild place I have not seen a priest but twice in thirty years. But every day during these thirty years have I prayed to God, that I might not die without the consolations of religion. He will not refuse this prayer—I know he will not; and, when I have a Catholic priest at my bedside to give me the last Sacraments, then I shall believe I am going to die, but not till then."

"My son," said the Bishop, "prepare yourself for death; I am a Catholic priest."

The holy rites were administered; the faithful soul slept in peace, and the good Bishop went on his way rejoicing, and praising God for his wonderful works towards the children of men.

THE THUNDERING LEGION

Marcus Aurelius, the Roman emperor, was engaged in a disastrous war with the Quadi, a warlike people living on the north of the Danube. His army had been hemmed in by the enemy within a narrow defile, and was, moreover, on the point of perishing for the want of water. Among his troops, however, were a large number of Christian soldiers, who, seeing the danger which threatened them, had recourse for help to the God of heaven. Kneeling on the ground, they poured out earnest entreaties to God to rescue the army and their emperor from destruction, by sending them a supply of water and enabling them to escape from their dangerous position. The enemy, and even their fellow-soldiers, stood amazed at this unexpected sight, but they were far more astonished at the speedy answer which God gave to their prayers. They had not been long on their knees, when suddenly the sky became dark, the wind howled through the forests, vivid flashes of lightning shot across the heavens and torrents of rain began to descend. The Roman soldiers first received the refreshing drops in their mouths, being ready to die with thirst; they then caught them in their helmets; but while they were so engaged, the enemy, wishing to overpower them in the storm, began the attack. The violence of the tempest was now turned upon the forces of the enemy. Blinded with wind and rain, they were unable to follow up the attack, and soon fled in disorder. The Romans, refreshed and strengthened, pursued them with great vigour, and gained a complete and decisive victory.

The pagan emperor justly attributed this victory to the prayers of his Christian soldiers, and they were from that time known by the name of the

Thundering Legion. In the city of Rome there may still be seen a column or pillar on which is carved a representation of this victory. The Romans are represented as fighting bravely with the enemy, and in the midst of the battle refreshing themselves with draughts of the falling rain. The enemy, on the contrary, are flying from the field of battle, where many lie stretched on the ground from the violence of the storm.

CONVERSION OF ST. JOHN GUALBERT

St. John Gualbert, a holy monk, and the founder of a religious order, may be said to have owed his conversion to an act of virtue, which he performed one Good Friday in honour of Jesus crucified. He was at that time a gay young nobleman, full of spirit and courage, but unhappily he cherished in his heart a bitter feeling of revenge against a neighbour who in a quarrel had killed his brother Hugh. John had determined to take the life of the murderer wherever he should find him, and was encouraged in this resolution by his father, who told him that this was the only way to wipe out the insult offered to the honour of the family.

While the young nobleman was occupied only with thoughts of revenge, and was eagerly seeking an opportunity for the commission of the deed, it happened that, riding to Florence upon Good Friday, he met the murderer in so narrow a passage that it was impossible for either of them to avoid the other. John, who was armed and attended by his servant, immediately drew his sword, and was going to despatch his enemy, when suddenly the latter, falling on his knees and stretching out his arms in the form of a cross, besought him, for the love of Jesus, who was crucified on that very day, to spare his life. The remembrance of Christ, who prayed for his murderers on the cross, exceedingly affected the young nobleman. He threw himself from his horse and gently raised the suppliant with his hand, saying, "I can refuse nothing that is asked of me for the sake of Jesus Christ. I not only give you your life, but also my friendship for ever. Pray for me that God may pardon me my sins." They then embraced each other and parted. Continuing his journey, John entered the first church that he came to, and, prostrating himself in prayer before a large Crucifix, begged with many tears that God would pardon his sins. Hereupon the crucifix bowed its head, as if in token that his prayer was heard, and that the generous sacrifice which he had made of his resentment was accepted by God. Attached to this church was a Benedictine Monastery, to which the young nobleman repaired, as soon as he had finished his prayer, in order to beg the favour of admission. His request was granted, and from that time he gave himself up entirely to prayer and works of penance, by which he made such rapid progress in virtue that he became an illustrious Saint and a bright ornament of the Church.

ST. MONICA AND THE SERVANT MAID

St. Monica, the mother of the great St. Augustine, was brought up under the care of a virtuous nurse, who earnestly endeavoured to train her in habits of self-denial as well as other virtues. Thus, among other excellent practices, she would never allow the little Monica to drink between meals, saying to her, "Now you only want a drink of water; but, when you grow up and are mistress of the cellar, you will not care for water, though the habit of drinking will still remain with you."

The very danger which the prudent servant had foreseen actually befell her, for as she grew older her parents frequently entrusted her with the key of the cellar, and sent her to draw the wine for the use of the family. When so doing she would sometimes out of curiosity take a little sip, but by degrees the quantity increased, and she acquired at length such a liking for wine that she would drink whole cupfuls with the greatest relish. Thus did she sow the seeds of the vice of intemperance, and expose herself by her self-indulgence to the danger of grievous excess. Almighty God saw her peril, and mercifully rescued her from the brink of the precipice in the following manner.

It happened one day that the young Monica had some angry words with one of the servants. Now this was the very maid who had been in the habit of accompanying her young mistress to the cellar, and had frequently noticed her fondness for the wine-cup. In her vexation she now reproached St. Monica with her failing, calling her a young wine bibber. This expression made the deepest impression on her mistress, who, entering into herself, sincerely deplored her fault, and from that moment entirely corrected it. Thus did her humility, in profiting by the rebuke of a servant, lay the foundation of her future sanctity.

AN INDIAN CHIEF ON DRUNKENNESS

Father de Smet, the zealous Jesuit Missionary of the North American Indians, praises the tribe of the Ravens for their determined opposition to the use of intoxicating drinks. "What good is this water of fire?" said their chief to the white man who sought to introduce among them the use of ardent spirits. "It burns the throat and the stomach; it renders man like a bear; as soon as he has tasted it, he bites, he grunts, he howls, and ends by falling down like a corpse. Your water of fire does nothing but evil; carry it to our enemies. They will kill each other, and their wives and children will be objects of pity. As for us we do not want it, we are mad enough without it."

FIRST COMMUNION OF THE BLESSED IMELDA

In the fourteenth century there lived at Bologna a holy virgin named Imelda, of tender years, but extraordinary piety. At the age of eleven, she had been admitted into the Dominican Convent of St. Mary Magdalen in that city, where she became the admiration of the community, on account of her exact observance of the rule, her spirit of penance, and the fervour of her devotion. Above all things it was her delight to spend hours in prayer before the Holy Sacrament, holding sweet converse with the Divine Spouse of her soul; and it was her longing desire to be admitted to his embraces in Holy Communion. This, however, had never yet been permitted by her confessor, on account of her tender years, though she frequently approached to the Sacrament of Penance, and had often and earnestly implored him to admit her to the Heavenly Banquet.

It happened one day, on the eve of our Lord's Ascension, that all the religious were approaching the altar to nourish their souls with the Immaculate Flesh of the Lamb of God, while Imelda alone was prevented from sharing in the Sacred Feast. On beholding the Divine Fountain of grace flowing so near, while she was excluded from quenching her ardent thirst with its living waters, Imelda was overwhelmed with grief, and kneeling towards the altar, poured out the longings of her soul at the feet of her Beloved, protesting that her only desire on earth was to be united to him in the Holy Sacrament. At the same moment, a Sacred Host was seen descending from above, until it remained suspended over the head of the holy virgin, who was now absorbed in an ecstasy of love. Her confessor, perceiving what had happened, ran to the spot, and taking with reverence the Host upon the paten, in obedience to this evident sign of the Divine Will, placed it on the tongue of the devout virgin. No sooner had she received the sacred particle, than the heavenly rapture of love, which consumed her soul at the possession of her Divine Spouse, burst asunder the ties which united it to the body, and she was borne in the embraces of her Beloved to the eternal sight and enjoyment of him in Paradise.

VIATICUM OF ST. JULIANA

St. Juliana Falconieri, a holy virgin who lived in the thirteenth century, was distinguished for her extraordinary devotion to Jesus in the Blessed Sacrament. In her last illness she earnestly desired to receive him in the Holy Viaticum, but on account of the continual sickness to which she was subject, it was considered impossible to comply with her pious desire. Moved, however, by her earnest entreaties, her confessor brought into her presence the Sacred Host, that she might have at least the consolation of adoring our Lord and receiving his last blessing. No sooner did she perceive the object of her ardent affection, than in a transport of love, forgetting her extreme weakness, she sprang from the bed, and cast herself on the ground to adore our Lord. Then with many tears she asked as a last favour, that since she could not receive Jesus sacramentally, his most Sacred Body might be laid upon her breast, that her heart might be refreshed by the near presence of him whom she so ardently loved. Her confessor, moved by her tears and entreaties, and knowing well the virginal purity of her soul and her eminent sanctity, granted her request, and a corporal having been spread upon the breast of the dying virgin, the Blessed Sacrament was placed upon it in the immediate neighbourhood of her heart. Scarcely had the priest laid the Sacred Host on the chaste bosom of Juliana, than overcome by the sweetness of our Lord's presence, and languishing with love, she cried out, "Oh, my sweet Jesus!" and expired. Wonderful to relate, the Sacred Host was no longer to be seen. In the last expiring act of love and longing desire, with which Juliana had greeted the presence of Jesus, the Sacred Host had passed into her heart, leaving as a convincing proof the impression of the Consecrated Particle upon her breast. Thus did Jesus satisfy the longing desire of this pure and loving soul, coming to her as her Viaticum, to accompany her to his heavenly kingdom.

THE EMPEROR NAPOLEON

The great Emperor Napoleon, in the days of his prosperity and his earthly glory, thought little of God, or of the practice of his religious duties. He was not, however, without faith, and afterwards, in the solitude of his captivity at St. Helena, became convinced of the vanity of the world, and returned to the practice of his religion. It was then that he made that beautiful answer to someone who asked him which had been the happiest day of his life. Was it the day of his victory at Lodi, or of that at Marengo; or was it rather the day of his triumphal entrance into Dresden or Vienna? "You are mistaken," he replied; "it was not any of these days, it was the day of my first Communion."

It happened one day that one of his officers, in his presence, impiously mocked at religion, and asked him, in a jesting way, how he could believe that there was a God, when he had never seen him. "Listen, and I will tell you," said Napoleon. "You say that I have a talent for war. When we used to go to battle, if there was any important movement to be made, you were the first to come and look for me, and every one cried out, 'Where is the Emperor?' And why so? It was because you trusted in my talent; yet you had never seen it. Did you, then, doubt its existence? No, because you had seen its effects. My victories proved that it existed, and thus no one called it in question. But which of my victories could be compared to any of the wonders of the creation, which all bear testimony to the existence of God? What military movement can bear any comparison with the movement of the heavenly bodies? My victories made you believe in me; the universe makes me believe in God."

THE PIOUS LABOURER

In the parish of Ars, in the time of its saintly curé or parish priest, John Baptist Vianney, lived a simple peasant, poor in the goods of this world and ignorant of its learning, but rich in piety and virtue. He was particularly remarkable for his ardent devotion to our Blessed Lord in the most holy Sacrament. Whether going to his work or returning from it, never did that good man pass the church door without entering it to adore his Lord. He would leave his tools, his spade, hoe, and pickaxe at the door, and remain for hours together sitting or kneeling before the tabernacle. The holy curé, who watched him with great delight, could never perceive the slightest movement of the lips. Being surprised at this circumstance, he said to him one day, "My good father, what do you say to our Lord in those long visits you pay him every day?" "I say nothing to him," was the reply; "I look at him and he looks at me."

ST. FRANCIS AND THE OLD MAN

We read in the life of St. Francis of Sales that he was one day giving Communion in a country Church, when an old man, whom he had communicated early in the morning, approached a second time to the altar rails. "My good friend," said St. Francis, "I have already given you our Blessed Lord; you must not come to receive him again." "Oh, my father," said the old man, "give him to me again, I beseech you; I felt so happy in his company." St. Francis could not help admiring the fervour and simplicity of the good old man, and as he could not grant his request he said to him, "Well, my friend, go away this time, but take care to come again tomorrow morning, and I promise you that I will give you our Blessed Lord once more." The old man went away consoled, and was punctual in returning again next morning, when he had again the happiness of receiving his God.

THE "ENCHANTED BREAD" OF THE CHRISTIANS

During the cruel persecution which raged against the Christian religion in the kingdom of Tong-Quin, under the tyrant Minh Menh, the grandfather of the present monarch, the power and efficacy of the Holy Eucharist in sustaining the courage of the martyrs was manifest even to the infidels. While these glorious champions of Jesus Christ were cruelly racked and scourged, or their flesh was torn off their bones with red hot pincers, the Holy Name of Jesus was ever on their lips, and they continued to profess their faith with undaunted courage. The Mandarins, amazed at a fortitude so far beyond the power of human nature, attributed it with truth to the Heavenly Food which the Christians partook of in their assemblies. "Truly," they would say, "this man has been eating of that enchanted bread which casts a spell upon the soul."

Among the other Christians who were about this time dragged before the tribunal and tortured for the faith, was a youthful hero named Xavier, a pupil of that illustrious martyr, Father Cornay. So extraordinary was his courage and intrepidity, that the Mandarin, who examined and subjected him to the torture, exclaimed, "Here is a youth, a mere boy, and yet he has the courage of a lion. What should I do, if I had to deal with a priest?" When he was led to execution the crowd repeated as he passed along, "See how he despises death. The Master of Heaven must certainly have descended and taken up his abode with him."

THE FIRST COMMUNION VEIL

A certain young girl, who had been brought up by virtuous and pious parents, had the happiness to make her first Communion with exceeding fervour and in the most excellent dispositions. The remembrance of the happy day on which she first received our Lord continued for a long time ever present to her mind, and became a powerful motive to encourage her to the practice of virtue. Every month she returned again to the Divine Banquet, and on her Communion days it was her frequent custom, when in private, to clothe herself again with the veil and wreath that she had worn on the occasion of her first Communion, in order that she might renew the sweet emotions which she had then experienced.

It happened, however, that as time went on, her fervour and piety relaxed. She grew lukewarm and slothful, careless about her prayers, and negligent in approaching the holy Sacraments, until she at last fell away by degrees into a worldly and sinful life. The sight of the garments which she had worn on the day of her first Communion now became hateful to her, for they never failed to awaken in her the voice of conscience, until at last, to avoid their continual reproach, she shut them up in a drawer which she seldom opened. Here they continued unnoticed for many years, during which this once innocent and holy soul fell deeper and deeper into the abyss of sin.

At length it pleased Almighty God to look upon her with eyes of mercy. Going one day by accident to the drawer where the veil and wreath had been laid by, she came upon them unexpectedly. Her first motion was one of impatience. "Cursed veil," said she, casting it on the ground, "can I never banish you from my sight! And yet," she added, for Divine grace began now to work in her heart, "how happy was I when first I wore you! Where is the innocence which then adorned my heart, where the robe of grace with which my soul was clad on that blessed morning when first I went to receive my God?" So saying, she knelt down and fervently kissed these tokens of her early innocence and piety. Then bursting into tears, she implored our Blessed Lord to pardon her many crimes and her past ingratitude, and restore her once more to his love and friendship. From that moment she quitted her evil life and became a sincere penitent.

THE DEVOUT COMMUNICANT

We read in the life of St. Aloysius Gonzaga, that being permitted by his Confessor to receive Holy Communion every Sunday, he divided the week between his thanksgiving and preparation, consecrating three days to each. The same is related of another devout soul who, in arranging his devotions, observed the following plan, which those who communicate weekly would do well to imitate. Sunday, the day of his Communion, was spent by him in sweet union and interior converse with our Blessed Lord. Monday was a day of thanksgiving for the rich treasure which he had received. On Tuesday he continually offered and consecrated himself to God. Wednesday was spent in constant petitions to his Divine Lord for all his own wants and for those of the whole Church. On Thursday he began his preparation for his next Communion, spending that day entirely in acts of faith and adoration: "Oh, my Jesus, I believe in thee, present in the most Holy Sacrament! Oh, my Jesus, I adore thee!" Friday was a day of humiliation and contrition, but of hope and confidence in the Divine mercy: "Lord, I am not worthy! Oh, Jesus, make me worthy! In thee have I hoped, and I shall never be confounded!" Finally, Saturday was devoted to acts of love and desire: "Oh, my Jesus, I love thee. I long for thee! Oh, my Jesus, come and take possession of me! My beloved to me and I to him!"

DEATH MAKES NO DISTINCTION

The holy Duke of Gandia, St. Francis Borgia, while in the world, occupied a high position at the court of the Emperor Charles V of Spain, and was particularly attached by him to the service of the Empress Isabella. On the occasion of her death, which happened in 1539, he was deputed to attend the body to Granada, where it was to be interred. Upon his arrival at that city, the coffin was uncovered, in order that Francis might certify on oath that it was indeed the body of the late Empress. But, behold! the countenance was to be no longer recognised, so hideous and disfigured was it by the ravages of death; while at the same time there issued from the corpse so frightful a stench that the spectators made haste to depart. Whereupon Francis cried out, "What is become of those eyes once so sparkling? Where is now the beauty and graceful air of that countenance which we so lately beheld? Are you her sacred majesty, Donna Isabella? Are you my Empress, my lady, my mistress? Thus, then," said he to himself, "end the greatness and the royal dignities of the world! Henceforth I will serve a master who can never die." From that moment he consecrated himself to the love of Jesus crucified, making a vow to become a religious, should his wife die before him. This vow he afterwards fulfilled, by entering into the Society of Jesus, then lately founded by St. Ignatius Loyola.

STORY OF JOSAPHAT

A prince, named Josaphat, had lost his way in a forest while hunting. Suddenly he heard some one, at a little distance, singing sweetly. Surprised to hear so lovely a voice in a lonely forest, he rode towards the spot from which the sound came, but was astonished to find that the voice which had so charmed him was that of a poor leper, whose body was in the last stage of decay. "Alas! my friend," said the prince, "how can you have the courage to sing in this dreadful condition?" "My lord," replied the leper, "I have every reason to rejoice. For forty years I have lived in this world, that is to say, my soul has been for forty years confined in this body, which is its prison. The walls of this prison are now falling to pieces, and my soul, set free from these ruins, will soon take her flight towards God, to enjoy, in his company, eternal happiness. I am so overjoyed at this thought that I cannot help raising my voice to heaven on this happy day of my deliverance."

THE MARTYRS OF JAPAN

During the cruel persecution raised by the Japanese Emperor Taicosama against the true religion, a glorious band of twenty-six Christians were condemned to suffer the barbarous punishment of crucifixion. Among this noble company of heroes were three young boys, the oldest of whom was not more than fifteen years of age. These generous youths showed no less courage than those who were more advanced in years; and the youngest especially, a boy of ten, named Louis, was remarkable for the extreme eagerness and joy with which he welcomed his cruel martyrdom. The Japanese general, touched with pity at his youth and amiable qualities, offered him, not only his life, but a place in his own household, on condition that he would abandon his religion; but Louis nobly answered, "On such a worthless condition as you propose, I reject the offer of life. Would you have me barter eternal happiness for a few fleeting years of temporal existence?" The same generous child, on arriving at the place of execution, as soon as the cross which was prepared for him, and which was smaller and shorter than the others, was pointed out, ran eagerly to it and stretched himself upon it, exclaiming, "Paradise, Paradise!" The same cheerful readiness was displayed by the rest of this noble band, who esteemed themselves happy to die for Jesus, and to die on the cross. Their hands and feet being secured to the wood by means of iron rings, according to the custom of the country, the crosses were raised in the air, and let fall into the holes which had been dug to receive them. On being raised aloft upon his cross, the young Antony, who had been taught by the Jesuit fathers to chant the Divine Office, began to intone the psalm "*Laudate pueri Dominum;* Praise the Lord, ye children." Meanwhile the rest of the holy martyrs encouraged each other, and exhorted the people, who stood in crowds to witness the moving sight. At length, at a given signal, the executioners approached, and, passing from one to another among the glorious band, pierced them with their spears, and thus set free their happy souls to fly to the embraces of their crucified God. This noble company of martyrs have been lately canonised by Pope Pius IX.

ST. FELICITAS AND HER SEVEN SONS

During the reign of the Emperor Antoninus, a noble Roman lady, named Felicitas, was brought before Publius, the prefect or governor of Rome, along with her seven sons, on a charge of practising the Christian religion. Publius, desirous of gaining over the children by means of the mother, took her aside, and earnestly entreated her to have pity on her children, and, by prevailing on them to offer sacrifice to idols, to save their lives and secure for them the favour and rewards of the Emperor. But the holy mother nobly answered, "Do not think to frighten me by threats, or to win me by fair speeches. The compassion you exhort me to would make me the most cruel of mothers. My children will live eternally with Christ if they are faithful to him, but must expect eternal death if they sacrifice to idols." Then, turning to her children, she said to them, "My sons, look up to heaven, where Jesus Christ with his Saints expects you. Be faithful in his love, and fight courageously for your souls."

The prefect, enraged, ordered her to be cruelly beaten, and then, calling her children before him, strove to induce them, both by threats and promises, to adore the false gods. The sons answered, with a spirit worthy of their mother, that they would never forsake Jesus Christ, and that they did not fear a passing death, but everlasting torments. The Emperor, being informed of their constancy, condemned each of them to a cruel death. The eldest was scourged to death with leaden plummets. The next two were beaten with clubs till they expired. The fourth was thrown headlong from a precipice. The three youngest, with the heroic mother, were beheaded.

THE YOUNG NIVARD

When St. Bernard and his three brothers were about to quit the world in order to serve God in the monastery of Citeaux, they first repaired to the Castle of Fontaines, to bid adieu to their aged father, and implore his blessing. As they came out of the gates of the castle, which is situated on the summit of a hill, they saw their little brother Nivard playing with other children of his age. "Good-bye, Nivard!" said Guy, the eldest of the brothers; "you will now be your father's heir, and one day master of all you see around. We leave to you all our possessions." "What!" said the child, with a wisdom beyond his years; "you take heaven for yourselves and leave me earth! Assuredly this division is not equal, and I shall very soon follow you." And so indeed he did when he grew older, for he also quitted the world, and entering the Abbey of Citeaux, put himself under the direction of his brother Bernard.

THE PRIEST AND THE BEGGAR

We read in the works of Thaulerus that there was a certain learned Divine, who had made it his continual prayer to God for eight years, that he would direct him to some man who would show him the true way in which to walk. At length on one occasion, when praying with extraordinary fervour, he heard a voice from heaven, which said to him, "Go to the church porch, and there thou shalt meet with a man who will show thee the way of truth." On going thither he found a poor beggar, whose feet were covered with sores and dirt, while all the clothes on his back were not worth three farthings. The priest, saluting him courteously, wished him a good morning. "Father," replied the beggar, "I never remember to have had a bad morning." "God prosper you," said the priest. "What say you?" replied the beggar, "I never was otherwise than prosperous." "I wish you all happiness," said the priest. "Why," said the poor man, "I never was unhappy." "God bless you," said the priest, "explain yourself, for I do not understand your meaning."

"I will do so willingly," answered the poor man. "You wished me a good morning, and I answered that I never had a bad morning; for if I am hungry, I praise God; if I suffer cold, I praise God; if it hail, snow, or rain, be the weather fair or foul, I give praise to God; if I am miserable and despised by the world, I still give praise to God; and, therefore, I never meet with a bad morning. You also prayed that God might prosper me, to which I answered, that I was never otherwise than prosperous; for I know for certain that all God does must needs be for the best, and, therefore, whatever happens to me by his will or permission, whether pleasant or disagreeable, sweet or bitter, I receive it with joy as coming from his merciful hand for the best—so that I was never otherwise than prosperous. You wished me also all happiness, and I in like manner replied that I had never been unhappy; for I have given up my own will to God so entirely, as only to will what he wills, and, therefore, I never was unhappy, having no desire to have any will except his."

HEROIC FAITH OF A CHILD

In the year 1833, a violent persecution was raised against the Church by the tyrant Minh Menh, king of Tong-Quin and Cochin China, and vast numbers were cruelly tortured and put to death for the faith. The Christians exhibited the most heroic constancy; even the very children nobly confessed the faith, and offered themselves to the judges to receive the crown of martyrdom.

One day a little boy, ten years old, presented himself at the tribunal. Throwing himself on his knees before the judge, he joined his hands, and asked permission to speak. "Mandarin," said he, "give me a cut with a sabre that I may go to my own country." "Where is your country?" said the judge. "It is in heaven," replied the child. "And where are your parents?" "They are gone to heaven, and I want to follow them. Give me a stroke with the sabre, and send me there." The mandarin was struck with admiration at the faith and courage of the child, but refused to grant his request. We may well believe that in after years this generous confessor of the faith took his place among that noble band of martyrs, who have since watered the soil of Tong-Quin with a continuous stream of blood.

THE FORTY MARTYRS OF SEBASTE

During the persecution waged against the Church by the Emperor Licinius at the beginning of the fourth century, a noble band of soldiers, forty in number, refused to join in the idolatrous sacrifices which were to take place in the camp by the Emperor's orders, and declared not only that they were Christians, but that they were ready to die for their faith. Promises and threats, as well as the most cruel torments having proved of no avail in shaking their resolutions, the judge condemned them to be stripped of their clothes and exposed naked, during a severe frost, upon a frozen pond. As an additional temptation he ordered a fire to be kindled and a warm bath prepared at a little distance, to which they might repair at any time when they were prepared to obey the Emperor's orders.

On hearing their sentence the martyrs ran joyfully to the place of their punishment, and, having undressed themselves, took their stand at once upon the ice, encouraging one another meanwhile to perseverance, by the reflection that one bad night would secure for them a happy eternity. Then raising their voices to God, they prayed with one accord, "Lord, there are forty of us engaged in this combat, grant that we may be forty crowned, and that not one may be wanting to this sacred number."

As night went on their sufferings became more intense, but they continued to pray fervently, nor did they show any disposition to yield, with the exception of one unhappy man, who leaving the pond, passed to the bath, which he had no sooner entered than he expired. Meanwhile one of the sentinels, who had been stationed before the fire, to observe whether any of the confessors consented to abandon his post, suddenly beheld the pond lit up with a heavenly light, and a band of Angels descending from above, who distributed rich garments and crowns among the generous confessors. He at once understood that the God of the Christians had sent this blessed company to reward the constancy and fidelity of his generous servants. At the same time, he wondered why there were but thirty-nine crowns prepared, whereas the soldiers numbered forty. While thus the sentinel pondered within himself, it was revealed to him that the man who had entered the bath, had forfeited the fortieth crown by his base apostasy, whereupon he was moved by an interior grace, and filled with an ardent desire of gaining it in his stead. He accordingly arose, stripped himself of his garments, and loudly proclaiming himself a Christian, took his place upon the ice amid the band of martyrs. Thus did God hear their prayer, though in a different manner from what they had expected; and when morning came, and the bodies of all alike, both living and dead, were cast upon a burning pile to complete their sacrifice, not one was wanting to complete that glorious company.

Additional titles available from

St. Augustine Academy Press
Books for the Traditional Catholic

Titles by Mother Mary Loyola:

Blessed are they that Mourn
Confession and Communion
Coram Sanctissimo (Before the Most Holy)
First Communion
First Confession
Forgive us our Trespasses
Hail! Full of Grace
Heavenwards
Holy Mass/How to Help the Sick and Dying
Home for Good
Jesus of Nazareth: The Story of His Life Written for Children
Questions on First Communion
The Child of God: What comes of our Baptism
The Children's Charter
The Little Children's Prayer Book
The Soldier of Christ: Talks before Confirmation
Trust
Welcome! Holy Communion Before and After

Titles by Father Lasance:

The Catholic Girl's Guide
The Young Man's Guide

Tales of the Saints:

A Child's Book of Saints by William Canton
A Child's Book of Warriors by William Canton
Illustrated Life of the Blessed Virgin by Rev. B. Rohner, O.S.B.
Legends & Stories of Italy by Amy Steedman
Mary, Help of Christians by Rev. Bonaventure Hammer
Page, Esquire and Knight by Marion Florence Lansing
The Book of Saints and Heroes by Lenora Lang
Saint Patrick: Apostle of Ireland
The Story of St. Elizabeth of Hungary by William Canton

Check our Website for more:
www.staugustineacademypress.com

Made in the USA
Monee, IL
19 October 2023